S·U·P·E·R
MEMORY

S·U·P·E·R
STUDENT

Also by Harry Lorayne

HOW TO DEVELOP A SUPER-POWER MEMORY

SECRETS OF MIND POWER

INSTANT MIND POWER

MIRACLE MATH

MEMORY ISOMETRICS COURSE

MENTAL MAGNETISM COURSE

GOOD MEMORY — GOOD STUDENT!

GOOD MEMORY — SUCCESSFUL STUDENT!

THE MEMORY BOOK

REMEMBERING PEOPLE

THE MAGIC BOOK

THE PAGE-A-MINUTE MEMORY BOOK

MEMORY MAKES MONEY

S·U·P·E·R MEMORY
S·U·P·E·R STUDENT

How to Raise Your Grades in 30 Days

H·A·R·R·Y LORAYNE

Little, Brown and Company
NEW YORK   BOSTON   LONDON

Little, Brown and Company
Hachette Book Group
237 Park Avenue, New York, NY 10017
Visit our Web site at www.HachetteBookGroup.com

Little, Brown and Company is a division of Hachette Book Group, Inc.
The Little, Brown name and logo are trademarks of Hachette Book Group, Inc.

Artwork by Robert E. Lorayne

Library of Congress Cataloging-in-Publication Data

Lorayne, Harry.
    Super memory — super student : how to raise your grades in 30 days /
by Harry Lorayne.
        p.   cm.
    ISBN 978-0-316-53268-6
    1. Memory.   2. Mnemonics.   I. Title.
LB1063.L63   1990
370.15'22 — dc20   89-12207

20   19   18

RRD-IN

Designed by Marianne Perlak

PRINTED IN THE UNITED STATES OF AMERICA

*To all those who have ever felt
the test/examination/schoolwork panic pangs,
and would prefer never to feel them again*

*And to Renée and Robert —
their love is my inspiration*

There is no learning
without memory.

Contents

• • •

S·U·P·E·R
MEMORY

S·U·P·E·R
STUDENT

Chapter 1

Toward Eliminating Study Panic

• • •

I know that the last thing you need is another book! There is, however, a world of difference between this book and all your others. This book will enable you to stop forgetting — to *know facts* that are in other books so that you may not have to carry around those books at all. I'm not talking about mundane things like forgetting to close the door, forgetting where you put your favorite pen, forgetting to make a promised phone call. I'm not talking about *just* forgetting. I want you to realize that *memory is knowledge.*

Memory is the stepping-stone to thinking, because without remembering facts, you cannot think, conceptualize, reason, make decisions, create, or contribute. **There is no learning without memory.** Be aware of that. I'm assuming you are aware of it — otherwise, you wouldn't be reading this book right now. There simply is no learning without memory. (An extreme example: you couldn't be reading this if you forgot your ABCs and the sounds made by those letters!) This particular book will teach you systems of memory that are easy and fun to learn and easy and fun to apply. They will be useful to you, not only for academics, but for the rest of your life.

These easy-to-learn systems will enable you to remember anything you want to remember in less than half the time it takes you now, retain it for as long as you like, and retrieve it whenever you need it. This means that you'll spend *less* time in order to know *more*, freeing up much time for you. People have doubled or tripled their test scores and their grade point averages using the systems taught in this book. Applying them will make life much easier for you, and will enable you to learn/remember facts when you hear or read them *the first time* — in or out of the classroom.

In an article in the *New York Times*, William J. Warren says that "private tutoring . . . appears to be used increasingly as a tool . . . to squeeze out as much of an edge as possible in the competition for admission to college." Parents are urging their children to get better grades, to turn their good transcripts into great ones. In the same article, Judith Langer, professor of education at the State University of New York at Albany, is quoted as saying, "B students are [in tutorial services] to become A students, and A students to become A+ students. There's greater stress among the middle class to be part of the upper class. Getting your child into a good college is part of that process."

That's what this book is all about — giving you that extra push, that extra edge. And you won't have to "cram" for hours every day in order to have it. You won't need tutoring; you'll know your work right away, when you originally hear it or read it, when you *first* study it. You won't have to cram at all.

Doing what you're doing right now — reading — is all you need to be able to do in order to learn and apply my systems of trained memory. This is not the kind of book to skim. You have to *read* it. Take the tests, do everything I tell you to do. I want you to be actively involved; I want you to answer questions, fill in blanks — *amaze* yourself.

And although I'm speaking primarily to high-school and college-level students, that does not mean that the techniques and systems aren't a great help to younger students; of course they are. They're a greater help than you can possibly imagine. Learning the multiplication tables, for example, is an excellent application. So, if you know an elementary- or middle-school youngster, help him (or her) learn these methods. What a marvelous way to start someone on the road to success!

With few exceptions, all memory work in high school and

college falls into three main categories: numbers; numbers in conjunction with names, words, or events; and reading material, which includes vocabulary and terminology. The techniques you'll learn are easily applied to these categories, and to the exceptions as well.

So, let's stop kidding around — you *know* that the better your memory is, the better your grades will be. All knowledge is based on memory; there cannot be one without the other.

You'll soon start to remember as you never have before, as you never dreamed possible. No, no — not a "better" memory, not an "improved" memory — but a memory you *never dreamed possible.* I wouldn't waste your time, or mine, for just "better" or "improved."

MEMORY:LEARNING:: (a) understanding:knowledge;
(b) knowledge:scholastic success; (c) memory:knowledge;
(d) understanding:memory; (e) learning:knowledge;
(f) understanding:learning

As a student, you know what the above paragraph is. It's the kind of question you'll find on the SAT (Scholastic Aptitude Test) and other tests of similar nature — achievement tests, the PSAT (Preliminary Scholastic Aptitude Test), the GMAT (Graduate Management Achievement Test), the LSAT (for law school), and so forth. What you have to do is find the closest "something" is to "something" as "memory" is to "learning."

Tutorial books suggest that you form a logical sentence that includes the two capitalized words, then repeat that same sentence, substituting the other possible choices. The pair of choices that fits — that makes sense — is the correct answer. *The Princeton Review* is highly rated in the school tutoring area; it also suggests that you first eliminate the obviously incorrect choices.

I threw you a curve with the above example — because you'll be hard put to find an *obviously* incorrect pair of choices. A logical sentence including the two capitalized words might be "Without MEMORY there is little LEARNING." Well, all six choices will "work." Think about them: Without understanding there is little knowledge. Without knowledge there is little scholastic success. Without memory there is little knowledge. Without understanding there is little memory. Without learning there is little knowledge. Without understanding there is little learning.

There are slight shades of difference, perhaps, but, generally speaking, they do all "work." A student wants, *needs*, good scores on these tests in order to help him or her get into the school of choice; and "choice" colleges can accept only 25 to 35 percent of those who apply for admission.

I became involved with memory training when I was in grade school. When I brought home a test paper with a low grade, my father punished me severely. So I had terrific motivation — *fear*. I soon realized that knowing the answers to the questions asked in those early school days had nothing to do with "smarts." If the question was "What's the capital of Maryland?" you either *remembered* that it's Annapolis, or you didn't. (Things haven't changed *too* much!)

I didn't have much patience for, or interest in, rote memory. So I looked for books on memory training. I found some dating back to the seventeenth century. I didn't understand 99 percent of the material (I was eleven years old!). But the 1 percent I did understand changed my life! And it will change yours. I twisted, manipulated, and invented (without realizing it) until the bits and pieces I'd found solved my personal memory (schoolwork) problems. I've invented, molded, streamlined through the years so that now I can show you how to solve *any* memory or study problem.

Man is the only animal that can laugh, blush, and remember. You already *have* "memory" ability, so I won't give you anything new; what I'll give you is a way to use what you already have in an entirely different, imaginative, creative, workable, fun way — and a way to reach the highest possible plateau.

Just memorizing something may not be precisely the same — nor as good or satisfying — as learning or knowing it. We're into semantics, "shadings," here. To me, the words "know," "learn," and "remember" are synonyms. Memory *is* knowledge; those are two magnets that cannot be separated. I'm not suggesting that memory is a substitute for understanding, application, or experience. But it surely is the most direct avenue to those desirable conditions and surely is the most important part of them.

I interviewed Looy Simonoff, associate professor of mathematics at the University of Las Vegas, and, on this point, he said: "Reasoning is reasoning about something. The 'something' is in the memory. And you won't understand something later if you don't *memorize* it originally. It's obvious, the more material in your memory, the more tools you have with which to reason, the more things you have to reason about. *To learn is to remember.*"

My memory systems will make your understanding *deeper*, your learning capacity *larger*, your joy of learning *keener*. The thrill, the enjoyment, that goes along with learning will stay with you all your life. I guarantee it — if you start applying the systems as you learn them.

Adam Robinson is the coauthor of numerous books, including *Cracking the System: The SAT*, part of a best-selling series of books on how to pass tests. He agrees that students *should* know how to use vocabulary words properly. He also says, "Oh, but for the SATs, all they *need* in order to pass is to remember as many words and their definitions as possible." (It's your *memory* that's being tested.)

I'll teach you how to do just that — easily. And as far as understanding goes, Adam Robinson says of my systems:

> They will help anybody. Also, your systems help students understand the material. It's not just remembering facts, it's understanding them. As you point out, it's easier to remember something that makes sense than something that doesn't. Many of your systems are designed to help students make sense of material — better retain it, better understand it."

Years ago, some educators pooh-poohed my systems. (Most of those educators are "in my camp" now.) They screamed that concepts were important, not memory. Now they agree that you'd better remember. Professor Simonoff says, "What good are concepts if you can't remember them?"

Francee Sugar is an educational therapist/consultant, a research associate at Robinson–De Hirsh Reading Clinic (New York City), and a reading and learning consultant for the Fisher-Landau program at the Dalton School (New York City). She says:

> Some teachers feel that if you understand a concept, then you'll be able to retrieve it, reconstruct it. But, a student might not be able to reconstruct anything if he can't remember it — even if he understands the concept. If he has to start at the very beginning and try to reconstruct something because he can't remember it — well, it's two strikes against him right away. Memory is a terrific tool; it enables you to reason because you can fall back on a foundation of data.

And, adds Adam Robinson: "Your systems *are* concepts, Harry. So, of course, they help the student remember concepts. Sure they do."

What you don't remember, you might as well not have learned.

Chapter 2

The Cross of Lorayne

• • •

*F*or years, I had to put up with teachers who insisted that memory and methods for remembering were not important. Yet those same teachers, when teaching music in the early grades, *always* helped their students remember/learn the lines of the treble clef (EGDDF) by suggesting that they think of the sentence "Every Good Boy Does Fine." And I wonder if there exists a teacher who hasn't at one time or another mentioned to students that it's easy to remember the shape of Italy because it looks like a boot.

Every high-school student I've spoken to knows about the acronym FOIL, which is a memory aid for remembering how to attack an algebraic equation: Firsts, Outers, Inners, Lasts. (More on this in the algebra section in chapter 20.) And I've never met a doctor or a medical student who didn't remember the cranial nerves (olfactory, optic, oculomotor, trochlear, trigeminal, abducens, facial, auditory, glossopharyngeal, vagus, accessory, hypoglossal) by reciting the couplet

> *On Old Olympia's Towering Top*
> *A Finn And German Vault And Hop.*

Professors have helped medical students learn the layers of the scalp by suggesting that the word "scalp" itself might remind them of skin, close connective tissue (cutaneous vessels and nerves), aponeurosis (epicranial), loose connective tissue, pericranium.

Well, what in the world are these ideas if not *methods for remembering and learning?* After you heard that Italy is shaped like a boot, you knew it — it became part of your knowledge. As did the lines of the treble clef once you heard, or *thought*, "Every Good

Boy Does Fine." Your teachers didn't help you learn other information this way because they didn't know how. Why else? They knew only the above (perhaps their teachers taught it to *them*), so they taught it to you. Now, some private schools teach my methods, and quite a few colleges make one or another of my books suggested or required reading.

I am interviewed in *Introductory Psychology* by Jonathan L. Freedman. Part of his commentary on my methods: "Other people, using his techniques, also have great memories. . . . Harry Lorayne is able to remember vast amounts of information and *can teach others to do so*. It is clear that he uses principles that have been *well documented by psychological research*." (The italics are mine.)

There are really only three *fundamental* learning skills:

1. Locating the information you need.
2. Remembering the information you locate.
3. Understanding and organizing the information you've located and remembered so that you can *apply* it.

This book is concerned with the large gap between step 1 and step 3. Your teachers help with step 1: they tell you which pages in which books to read and learn (remember). Step 3 usually entails on-the-job training. But the teaching of the basic skill of remembering information is usually ignored. It hasn't always been: Simonides (circa 500 BC) used, taught, and wrote about trained memory systems. Aristotle, Cicero, Plato, and Socrates, among others, taught and used and wrote about the art of memory. Through the mists of time, scholars have improved, enlarged, and used systems of memory. I stand on the shoulders of giants — and there's room for you to stand there with me!

All right, then; I want you to get over that "hump" of memorizing your schoolwork, that ordinarily boring (to the point of tears), time-consuming drudgery, so that you can more quickly — *amazingly* more quickly — get to the nitty-gritty: the understanding, learning, applying, creating, thinking, reasoning, contributing! And still have more free time than you've ever had before.

I've said it so many times, it's been copied so many times, I may as well say it again: The "three R's" cliché — reading, 'riting, 'rithmetic — should be four R's. The first R should be *remembering*. Because without that first R, you can't read, write, or do 'rithmetic! All education is based on remembering. I know of no high school or college subject that doesn't require lots of memory work. Please, *please*, Mr. and Ms. Teacher, tell me what "studying" means if it doesn't mean *memorizing*. Can't you see, Mr. and Ms. Educator, that knowing how to remember is (along with knowing how to read) the core, the heart and soul, of learning and education? Can't you see that it's the fundamental premise for all students, at any level, throughout their school careers? Gimme a break. Give the students a break. "Memory" is spelled with six letters; it is *not* a four-letter word. Help me shed that cross — admit that methods for remembering are extremely important. *Teach* your students how to remember quickly, easily, definitely, thoroughly, creatively, imaginatively, in a *fun* way. You won't? You can't? Okay. *I will*, because *I can*.

Chapter 3

Start Remembering and Studying "Smart"

• • •

*U*sing memory properly is a skill and an art, and it must be learned from the beginning; there are no shortcuts at first. (My systems *are* the shortcuts.) The techniques will be new and foreign to you, a way of thinking that may seem silly at first. Don't make the mistake of deciding something is silly because you've never heard of it. Once you get past the fundamentals, you'll realize how practical, fascinating, and *non*-silly the systems are (particularly since you'll see results as you move through those fundamentals).

It is important for you to know that the secret of a good or incredible memory is *Original Awareness*. When someone says he forgot something, it usually means he never remembered it in the first place. You can't forget something you never knew; but anything that registers in your mind in the first place is easy to recall and just about impossible to forget.

That's what I mean by Original Awareness — forcing information to register in your mind or memory *in the first place*. Applying the systems will *force* you to be Originally Aware of any information the first time you see, hear, or read that information.

The one rule that holds true for all memory, trained or untrained, is: **In order for you to remember any new thing, it must be associated with something you already know or remember.** Association, pertaining to memory, simply means the tying together or connecting of two or more things.

That rule is the crux, the basis, of all memory. You've used association all your life. Memory exists because of it. Anything you've ever remembered you have associated with something else — as in the "Italy-boot" and "EGBDF–treble clef" examples. When you see or hear something that makes you say, "Oops, that reminds me," you're using association; one thing is somehow connected to the other. That's *why* it "reminds" you.

The problem is, you do it subconsciously, without thinking about it, realizing it, or having control over it. Your goal, now, is to *knowingly and consciously* — with control — be able to associate anything you want to remember with some other thing that will *remind* you of it. The *Link* and *Peg* systems of memory will enable you to do just that.

Abstract or intangible information is much more difficult to remember than concrete, tangible, and meaningful information. The *Substitute Word* technique will solve that problem for you by making abstract information tangible and meaningful *in your mind*.

These, then, are the techniques you will be using: the Link, Peg, and Substitute Word systems of memory. With them, you will be able to memorize *any* schoolwork with ease. Compared to the way you've been cramming now, you will soar through your work! To quote *Cracking the System* coauthor Adam Robinson further: "Another thing that your systems show and teach is just how to develop a system on a student's own. I mean, a student can think, 'Gee, anything can be broken down; there are easier approaches.' There's a thing called studying smart, Harry; you teach people how to remember smart." (He's talking about applying *strategies* for learning. Remedial therapist Francee Sugar agrees: "Strategies are very, very important, and the ability to develop and use them is intrinsic to learning. You need strategies to improve your memory. Learning-disabled students are too often at a loss on how to develop strategies on their own. Your systems are marvelous strategies.)

To "remember smart" you must understand the Link and Peg systems. I'll teach them to you in "stunt" form. As you learn and practice them, you may not see how they apply to your studies. They do; but learn the fundamentals first, then apply them to your work — and you'll be doing that in an extraordinarily short time.

You may want to show off for family and friends with the fundamentals. There's nothing wrong with that; do it. It's good practice. Make a game out of it. See how many things you can remember after you learn the ideas. Do it for fun. It *is* fun.

To remember — that is, *know* — the names of the five Great Lakes, picture (*imagine*) many HOMES on a lake. HOMES will remind you of Huron, Ontario, Michigan, Erie, Superior. Do you need to remember them by ascending size? Picture hills on lakes; there's a man on each hill. On Each Hill Man Stands. Ontario, Erie, Huron, Michigan, Superior.

Silly? Sure. But it works! Acronyms can come in handy once in a while. Some high-school students remember the different forms of energy by thinking of the word "McHales." If familiar with the energy forms to begin with, "McHales" would remind of mechanical, chemical, heat, atomic, light, electrical, and solar. The problem, of course, is that the student might not remember that word when asked about forms of energy. That problem is solved by applying the Substitute Word System, as you'll see.

Medical and dental students know that the human bite requires five muscles. If they know the names of those muscles in the first place, BITEM is a good *reminder:* Buccinator, Internal pterygoid, Temporal, External pterygoid, Masseter.

I know that some reference books say Japan's Mount Fuji is 12,365 feet high because I visualized the mountain made up of millions of calendars. Calendar reminded me of 12 months and 365 days in a year — 12,365 feet. The problem is that I've yet to find anything else that's 12,365 feet high, wide, or deep!

The above are helpful, but too limited; they apply to (and work for) specific things only. I want you to be able to associate (remember) *anything*. You'll learn systems that are unlimited in scope, that can be applied to any kind of information, at any time, under any circumstances.

Here comes the good stuff, now!

Chapter 4

The Link System of Memory

• • •

Remember as You Never Have Before

*T*he first thing is for you to see how simple it is to apply the rule I mentioned earlier: **In order for you to remember any new thing, it must be associated, *in some ridiculous way,* with something you already know or remember.** Note, please, the addition of the phrase *in some ridiculous way.* Those four words, that *concept,* is my contribution to the rule and that's what makes it fun. More important, that's what makes it *work.*

Ordinarily, if I asked you to memorize, say, ten items in sequence after hearing or reading them only once, you'd think it impossible. And you'd be right! Ordinarily, you couldn't do it. But learn to apply the rule, and a few other simple ideas, and you'll see how *easy* it is. The Link System of memory is designed to enable you to remember any number of things in sequence.

I'll use these ten items as examples: lamp, paper, bottle, bed, fish, telephone, window, flower, nail, typewriter. We'll make ridiculous mental pictures or associations between or with two items at a time, until we've associated, or *Linked,* all ten of them. C'mon along — it's easy and it's fun!

The first thing to do is get a picture of the first item, "lamp," in your mind. Just "see" a lamp in your mind's eye. If you want to visualize a familiar lamp, one you have at home, fine; do so. At first, something familiar will be easier to picture; after a while, it simply won't matter.

If we make a couple of assumptions, we can start to apply my rule now. Assume that lamp is the thing you *already* remember, and also that the *new* thing, the thing you want to remember, is "paper." All right; associate lamp with paper. That is, form a ridiculous picture involving both those items. The picture *must* be ridiculous — or *impossible*. You want an impossible "happening" between the two things; make it as crazy or silly as you like.

You might see a picture in your mind of a gigantic sheet of paper with a string attached. You pull the string and the paper lights up like a lamp! Or, you might see yourself writing on a lamp instead of on paper. Or, a gigantic sheet of paper is lighting a lamp. Or, a lamp is writing on a sheet of paper. Do you see what I mean?

There are many ways to form ridiculous associations between any two items. *Don't* use a logical picture. A logical picture, the kind not to use, might be that of a sheet of paper lying near a lamp. That's possible, logical, probable — and it won't work.

Okay; the next step is to see clearly in your mind for a split second or so the picture you've selected, or a picture you thought of yourself. Really see that picture; imagine it actually happening. Stop reading right now for a few seconds and *see* the impossible picture you've selected of "lamp" and "paper." Do it now.

The only way you'll know whether or not this works is if you try it. Bear in mind that even if the idea doesn't work, just *trying* to apply it *must* better your memory. From now on, whenever I tell you to "see the picture," stop reading and *really see that picture* in your mind's eye.

If you've seen that picture, stop thinking about it now. Let's continue. The next item to remember is "bottle." You have to form a ridiculous association (picture) between "paper" and "bottle." Do not think about "lamp" at all for now.

You might see paper pouring out of a bottle instead of liquid. Or, a gigantic bottle is made of paper; or a large sheet of paper is drinking from a bottle. Select one, or use a picture you've thought of yourself (as long as it's ridiculous or impossible), and, most important, *see that picture* in your mind for a second. Do it now.

"Bed" is the next item. You have to associate bottle with bed. Try to think of your own silly picture. This is an individual and personal thing; it will work much better if you think of your own pictures. When you do, you are concentrating on those two items, or pieces of information, as you never have before. *The very act of trying to associate will lock those items into your memory!*

I'll give you suggestions for pictures all the way through, however, because this is the first time you're trying this. See a gigantic bottle sleeping in a bed.

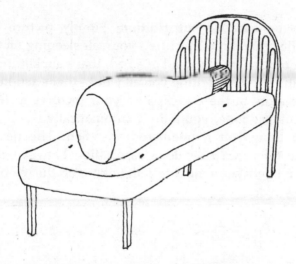

Or, you're sleeping in a gigantic bottle instead of a bed. Or, millions of bottles are piled up on your bed. Select one of those silly pictures — and *see* it in your mind's eye.

The next item is "fish." You can use the same ideas. See a large fish sleeping in a bed, getting the bed all wet. Or, you're fishing and catch a bed! Take a second to see whichever you think is sillier. You might have thought of a bed fishing. Fine. *See* it.

I realize that forming ridiculous pictures may seem a bit strange. That's all right. If you have to make a slight effort in order to form those silly pictures, that's *good*. That bit of effort will help you at first. There are four simple ideas that will help make your pictures silly or impossible. One is to see an item larger than life — **out of proportion.** That's why I've used the word "gigantic" in some examples, to force you to do just that.

Another way is to **exaggerate the number** of items. You might have pictured a *million* fish on a bed. Also, try to get **action** into your picture. Action is easier to remember. If you pictured a million pieces of paper (exaggeration) flying out of the lamp and hitting you in the face (hurting you), that would be action (or violence).

Finally, you can use **substitution.** Simply picture one item *instead of* the other. If you pictured yourself sleeping on a gigantic (out-of-proportion) fish instead of a bed, that's substitution. If that fish was biting you, or getting you all wet — that's action. You can get one or more of these ideas into your pictures to help make them ridiculous. Soon, you'll do it automatically.

The last thing you remembered was fish. The new item is "telephone." Form a ridiculous association between those two things. You might see a gigantic fish talking on the telephone and dripping as it does.

Or, you're talking into a fish instead of a telephone. Or, you're talking on the phone and a million fish fly out of it and hit you.

(Note that there's at least one of the four rules in each picture.) Select one ridiculous image and, most important, see that picture.

The next item is "window." See a silly picture of telephone and window. Visualize yourself tossing a gigantic telephone through a closed window and smashing that window into a million pieces. Or, see a window making a telephone call. Be sure to see the picture you select.

Next item — "flower." You might see windows growing in a garden instead of flowers — see yourself watering them. Or, you open your window and millions of flowers fly into your house. See the picture.

"Nail" is next. You're hammering a large flower into the wall instead of a nail.

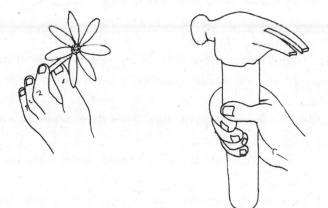

(Soon you'll see that the illogical picture comes to mind before a logical one does!) Gigantic nails are growing instead of flowers, or a gigantic nail is watering flowers. I could go on and on with examples — but all you need is *one* picture. See it in your mind's eye.

The last item is "typewriter." You're hammering a gigantic nail through a new typewriter, ruining it. Or, all the keys on your typewriter are nails, points up, and you hurt yourself as you type. Or, a gigantic nail is typing. Don't think that because this is the last item, you'll remember it "anyway"; you won't if you don't make the association. So *see* the picture.

Have you tried to see all the pictures in your mind? If not, go back and do it now. Then, get ready to amaze yourself! You now know (remember) all ten items, in sequence. Do you want to try it? Okay. Use a pencil; fill in the blanks that follow. Try not to look ahead as you fill in each blank.

You probably know the first item, but since I haven't as yet told you how to handle that (I will below, in the question-and-answer section), I'll tell you what it is. The first item is "lamp." Think of that for a moment. What does it make you think of? What crazy or silly thing were you doing with a lamp, or what ridiculous thing was a lamp doing? Perhaps something else was *being* a lamp. Lamp should remind you of _____.

If you wrote "paper" in the blank, you're correct. Now, think of paper; what does *that* make you think of? Paper should remind you of _____.

"Bottle," right! Think of bottle for a moment. Now what does that remind you of? What ridiculous thing was the bottle doing? Bottle reminds you of _____.

It should have reminded you of "bed." Now think of bed for a moment. That must lead you to _____.

"Fish" is correct. Think of fish, which should almost force you to think of _____.

Yes, that's right — "telephone." And telephone makes you think of _____.

If you wrote "window," you're absolutely right. You've made good ridiculous pictures. Window will remind you of _____.

Yes, of course — "flower." What were you doing with that flower, or what was growing instead of flowers? Perhaps you were hammering a flower instead of a _____.

"Nail" is correct. And, finally, nail should remind you of _____.

That's it — "typewriter." Did you fill in all the blanks? Correctly? If you want to shout "Wow!" go ahead — I know how you feel. You should be proud of yourself. You've done something most people can't do — memorized, learned, ten items in sequence after reading them only once.

If you hesitated over one or two, it's okay. Just go back and strengthen that particular association; that is, make sure the picture is ridiculous enough and, more important, be sure to *see* it clearly. You need to see that picture for only a second or less. It's not the length of time that's vital, it's the clarity of the picture that's important. See if you can list all the items from "lamp" to "typewriter" on your own. I know you can, so I want you to; I want to build your confidence. Take the time to do it — now.

Next, try this: Think of typewriter. That reminds you of what? Nail, of course. Think of nail, and that reminds you of . . . flower. Right. Flower makes you think of . . . sure, window. Think of window and you're automatically reminded of . . . telephone. Telephone should make you think of . . . fish. Right! Fish reminds you of . . . bed. Bed makes you think of . . . bottle. Bottle leads you to . . . paper. Finally, paper will remind you of . . . lamp.

Do you realize what you've just done? You knew the list of items *backward*. There's no need for you to remember your schoolwork backward, of course. I just want to show you how well the idea works. And doing it backward when you're showing off is impressive; it's "cool."

I call this the Link System because you're forming a chain that Links the items you want to remember. You can retain such a list for as long as you want to, or as long as you need to remember the information. All you'd have to do is go over the Link mentally every once in a while. It takes no time at all. Once you've memorized information this way, each use of that information, each application, will be an automatic review. When you've used the information three or four times, no more review is necessary. The silly pictures will fade; you won't need them anymore. The memorized material has become *knowledge*.

If you can remember a list of 10 items, you can remember a list of 15 or 16 items. If you can remember 15 or 16, you can memorize

25 or 26. There is really no limit. It will, of course, take longer to Link, say, 50 items than it will to Link 15 or 16. But it'd take longer to do that whether or not you applied the Link System!

Let me stress that just trying to apply the Link System to a list of items *forces* you to pinpoint your concentration on two items at a time in a way that you never could before. It *focuses* your concentration, forces Original Awareness. The information *must* register in your mind when you apply this idea.

The Link is used, basically, to help you remember things in sequence only. There are many kinds of information that must be memorized/learned in sequence, at least at first, when you begin to study it. I'll be giving many examples of just that in this book. The Link System of memory will help *immeasurably*. Practice it, learn it, understand it. Then, after you've tried it by yourself, a good way to continue to practice is to demonstrate your new memory power for family and friends. Ask someone to call out some objects and have him write them down. Let him call out 15 or 16, or as many as you feel you can handle comfortably.

He must write them down for two reasons. First, of course, is that that's the only way he'll be able to check you. Second, the writing gives you the time you need to make good, strong associations.

After he's listed the 15 or 16 items, call them off, in sequence, from first to last. If you miss one or two, don't panic. Ask him to tell you what they are, strengthen that particular association, and then call them off backward. You sure will impress him! Try it; see for yourself — but before you do show off with the idea, I'd suggest you try the practice lists at the end of this chapter. Also, do the drills and read the short question-and-answer section.

I want you to understand the ideas thoroughly before you tackle your schoolwork (although you'll be doing that sooner than you think). It may take a bit of time for you to become thoroughly familiar with the ideas, but before you know it, they'll be saving you time. *Learn the systems in order for them to help you learn.*

Questions and Answers

I've been teaching these ideas long enough to pretty much be able to pinpoint the questions that you may want to ask. Let's see if I can anticipate some of them.

Q. How do I remember the first item of a Link?

A. For the time being, associate that first item with *yourself* in some ridiculous way. That will do it. Or, associate the first item with the friend for whom you're showing off. When applying the idea to study material, the main subject itself will lead you into the Link. Of course, another way is simply to start at any item (near top) in the Link and work backward. That *must* bring you to the first item.

Q. How many items can I remember using the Link system?

A. There's really no limit. Since one item will always lead you to the next, it doesn't matter how many items there are. Of course, the longer the list, the more often you'll want to review it mentally.

Q. Is it all right to form a "story" in my mind that Links the items?

A. No, it isn't! Each pair of items should be handled as a separate entity. Trying to include all the items in one picture story may confuse you. Each association should concern itself with only the two vital items. A kind of story will form anyway, but form each association as taught — a separate and distinct picture for each pair of items.

Q. Why must the pictures I form in my mind be silly or ridiculous?

A. We usually forget mundane, everyday, ordinary things. The ridiculous-picture idea takes anything *out* of the "mundane." Forming a logical picture requires too little thought. What you don't think of, for at least a split second, cannot really be remembered. Making the pictures ridiculous *forces* you to *think* of the items. It forces Original Awareness. Applying the Link idea using logical pictures wouldn't work nearly as well.

Q. Will it confuse me if the same item appears in different lists or if an item repeats within the same list?

A. Good question. The answer is that you can memorize as many lists as you want using the Link System. The same item in more than one list will not confuse you. You need only try it to see that this is so. And if an item appears more than once within a list, no problem. Simply form the pictures as taught; they'll be different enough to act as the necessary reminders.

Q. How long can I retain a list that I've memorized with the Link System?

A. Any list of any kind of information can be retained for as long as *you* want to or need to retain it. We have to assume that, except for practice or showing off or "knowledge for knowledge's sake," any list you memorize is to be *used*. It is that use that forces retention. Once the information is etched into your mind, when it becomes *knowledge*, the original associations or pictures fade; you no longer need them. The information will stay with you for as long as you need it.

Q. What if a friend calls out abstract or intangible things?

A. Tell him to call tangible items only. Don't let him control you — you control him. Remember; *you're* demonstrating for him. If he refuses, just don't demonstrate for him (it's his loss, right?). It's really academic, because you'll soon be able to handle intangible things as easily as tangible things. Then, the problem ceases to exist.

Q. If I memorize a list via the Link System that I don't intend to use for a while, will that information fade?

A. Yes, part of it will — unless you review it mentally every so often. I mean once every three days, then once a week or so. The review takes no time, it's a mental exercise, and it will etch the information into your memory so that you'll know it *when you need it*.

Q. I can't wait to apply the idea to schoolwork. When can I do that?

A. Actually, if you had to remember a list of concrete, tangible things, you could start right now, couldn't you? But here's a better answer to your question: How about right after you do the drills that follow?

Complete These Drills — Have Some Fun!

Here are four lists of items. Memorize each one via the Link System of memory. Be sure to make each picture ridiculous, and see each ridiculous picture in your mind's eye for a split second. Remember the four rules for forming ridiculous or impossible pictures: *out of proportion, exaggeration, action, substitution.* Don't do all the lists at one sitting. Give your mind a rest between lists.

drum	pin	feather	airplane
string	window shade	snake	tea bag
gum	glass	belt	soap
key	desk	cup	telephone
paint	car	eyeglasses	foot
light bulb	pipe	building	garbage can
ball	stamp	comb	dog
picture frame	cage	scissors	pen
cracker	ice cube	cuff links	plate
record player	pizza	elephant	ring
chair		bed	lamppost
shark		doughnut	cards
coin			stapler
baby			sled
briefcase			paper bag
			dress
			fork
			tree
			magazine
			teeth

After you've done the four lists — and I want you to do them, to prove to yourself that you *can* — you can make up your own for more practice. Then, you're ready to show off for a friend.

Here's a final drill. Jot down three ridiculous-picture ideas for each of the following pairs of items. The purpose of this drill, of course, is to practice forming ridiculous pictures quickly. It's also a great imagination exercise! *Don't* use logical pictures. I've started you off. Turn the page and complete the drill.

toothbrush and guitar	Brushing your teeth with a guitar.
rock and pencil	
microphone and book	
lamp and necktie	
baseball bat and rubber band	
ship and paper clip	
tin can and wheel	

buzz saw
and
coffeepot

_____

_____

_____

cigar and
dollar bill

_____

_____

_____

doorknob
and bean

_____

_____

_____

scale and
letter

_____

_____

_____

newspaper
and marble

_____

_____

_____

calendar
and couch

_____

_____

_____

hair and
blotter

_____

_____

_____

cake and
matchbook

_____

_____

_____

You should have had fun with this. If you want some more practice, simply move all the second items up one step. Then you'll be working with toothbrush and pencil, rock and book, and so on. Switch them around any way you like in order to get different pairs of items with which to work.

If you completed the drills without too much trouble, you're ready to continue. If you had a bit of trouble, please reread the chapter, then try the drills again before you continue.

Chapter 5

Studying with
the Link

• • •

$\mathcal{O}$nce you've completed the "ridiculous-pictures" drill, you're ready to take another giant step toward remembering (studying) better, more easily, and with more fun and imagination — toward *"remembering smart."*

I have a stack of examples taken from high-school and college textbooks, given to me by students as they wailed, "Oh boy, if I could only remember this quickly, and retain it!" I've pulled out one of those examples, and I'll be "pulling out" other examples throughout this book. This one is a "hardness scale." Everyone who studies geology must, in order to be able to identify minerals, memorize this type of list; it consists of ten minerals *in sequential order.* And in my source, an old teacher's edition of a textbook on earth science, each one is given a hardness number from 1 to 10. Students tell me that they'd better know (remember) them "by number," too. We'll get to that soon enough. Right now, since you've just learned how to remember items in sequence, let's stay with that.

Here's a version of a hardness scale (it lists ten minerals in increasing order of hardness and enables the student to determine scratchability):

1. talc
2. gypsum
3. calcite
4. fluorite
5. opalite

6. feldspar
7. quartz
8. topaz
9. corumdum
10. diamond

(NOTE: In some textbooks and references I checked, the fifth mineral, opalite, is given as "apatite" or "opaline," feldspar is listed as "orthoclase," and corumdum is spelled "corundum." I found slight differences in other printed technical information while preparing this book. So, you may see an example or two here that differs a bit from what you are being taught. No matter, of course. I want you to understand the *techniques;* then you'll be able to apply them to any information *you* want to learn.)

The problem: Memorize the minerals in sequence, talc to diamond. The solution: Apply the Link System of memory. But wait a moment — how can we? We can't visualize things like "talc," "gypsum," and so on. Oh yes, we can. The Link is based mainly on the *reminder principle.* I've taught you to force one thing to remind you of the next. This is a natural phenomenon, something you have done and will do many times, all through your life. You see something that makes your mind snap its fingers and say, "Oops, that reminds me!" It's a natural, subconscious mental calisthenic over which you have no control. I've taught you to apply the reminder principle consciously, *with* control. The ridiculous picture *forces* one thing to remind you of another.

Let's enlarge on that idea just a bit. What does "talc" make you think of? Brainstorm it for a moment. How about "talk?" That sounds almost like the word "talc," doesn't it? So does "take," or even "tall k [the 'k' sound]." Of course, it may make you think, simply, of "powder" (talcum). Yes, "talc" could make you think of — *remind* you of — any of those things. And here's the crucial part: any of those things would also *remind you of "talc"!*

So, you *can* visualize "talc," because visualizing "talk," "take," "tall k," "powder" — anything *you* think of as a reminder, as a *substitute* — is the *same as* visualizing "talc," because it will automatically remind you of it! Once you understand this principle, you can apply the Link System to these minerals, just as you applied it to more concrete items like lamp, paper, bottle, and so forth. Let's do it; work along with me.

Use whichever substitute picture (or word) you like to remind you of talc. I'll assume, for teaching purposes, that you're "seeing" *powder*. *Powder* has to be associated, as you've already learned, to the next item. The next item is *gypsum*. What can you use to remind you of that? Well, what does it sound like? How about *gyp some*, *gyps 'im*, *gypsy*? If *you* thought of it, it *must* remind you of — it's really the *same as* — gypsum. (*Chip sum* or *chip some* would also work.) So, associate *powder* to, say, *gypsy*; form a ridiculous picture between the two items. Perhaps you'll visualize a gigantic gypsy (see whatever the word conjures up in your mind) pouring powder all over everyone, all over the world. Use that, or a picture you thought of yourself, and, as you know, *see* it in your mind. Do it; work with me.

You want *gypsum* to remind you of *calcite*. *Call sight, calls height, cold site* would remind you of that. (Do you know anyone named Cal? His height — *Cal's height* — or his skin — *Cal's hide* — would do fine.) So, perhaps someone is measuring heights and a gypsy calls out those heights — *gypsy, calls height*. (Remember, I don't care how silly you get.) See that picture.

Floor right will certainly remind you of *fluorite*, particularly if *you* thought of it. (My helping you is not really helping you. It all works better if you think up your own reminders and pictures. As mentioned, however, I have no choice but to give you suggestions at the beginning.)

Someone is calling heights (*calcite*) and the *floor* yells "*right*" each time. See that picture, or one you thought of yourself.

Now you need something to remind you of *opalite*. There are many ways to go — *opal light, oh pal light, oh polite, open light*. Associate *floor right* to one of those; perhaps a floor keeps saying "right" to everything because it's *oh* so *polite*. See the picture; *think* of it for a second.

You want *opalite* to "bring you to" *feldspar*. *Felled star* is what I see to remind me of feldspar; it's close enough in sound. (*Field spar, fell spear, felt spear, felled* while *sparring*, are all good, too.) You're being oh so polite to a felled (fallen) star.

See the silly picture that *only you can see.*

More rapidly now: A *felled star* looks like a gigantic *quarter* (quartz), or *quarts* of liquid pour out of a felled star. Or, you *felt* a *spear* and *quarts* of liquid pour out and soak you. See the picture.

Connect *quarter* or *quarts* to *toe pass, to pass,* or *dope ass* (donkey). One of these will remind you of *topaz.* Perhaps you see yourself pouring quarts of liquid over a dopey ass. See it.

The dopey ass eats a gigantic apple *core* that's soaked in *rum,* and that makes him *dumb.* Core rum dumb — *corumdum.* See the picture.

A gigantic apple *core* (just that is enough of a reminder; *corps* would do, too) is around your finger — it's a *ring* (to remind you of *diamond*). Or, the core sparkles like a diamond, or it is playing cards and holds the ace of diamonds. Select a picture and see it, *imagine* it.

Explaining what goes on in the mind takes much longer than what actually goes on in the mind. I've had to use time and space to teach you how to Link the ten minerals. Had you known the system, you could have memorized the list in a *fraction* of the time that it took me to explain it.

Right now, test yourself; see if you know the hardness scale. Start with talc (powder) and glide to the end. Try it; fill in these blanks:

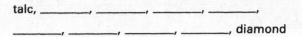

talc, _____, _____, _____, _____,

_____, _____, _____, _____, diamond

And yes, you know them backward, too. If you're studying geology, or if you will be studying it, you're ahead of the game. Obviously, if you want to remember "apatite" or "opaline" rather than "opalite," use *appetite* or *open line* (or *oh pal lean*) as your substitute thought instead of *oh polite*; if you want to remember orthoclase, use *oar tow class* instead of *felled star*; and for corundum, use *run* instead of *rum* in the proper pictures. You might, incidentally, want to start your Link with *hard scale* to tell you what the list is. (You could see yourself sprinkling lots of talcum powder on a very large, hard scale.) And, you'll soon learn how to remember/know the ten minerals *by number*.

Chapter 6

Numbers

• • •

Remember Them Now and Forever

*I*f you've attempted to do what I've asked you to do up to here (if you haven't, go back; *don't* continue reading), you should be amazed and pleased with yourself. But "you ain't seen nothin' yet!"

According to *The Guinness Book of World Records*, the Yancos, members of a primitive Amazon tribe, can count only up to three. And, their word for "three" is *poettarrarorincoaroac*. Now, *there's* a memory problem! And can you imagine the problem it'd be if they could count to twelve? Well, you can count to an infinite number but, more important, when you know how, you can *remember* to an infinite number.

Onward, then, toward that goal. You see now that it's not a large problem to memorize information in sequence, and that's fine. But what if you've memorized such a list and you'd like to know quickly, say, the seventh item? Quickly now, what's the seventh mineral of the hardness scale? Do you see what I mean? You know it, but you have to take the time to count to it, either from the top of your list, or from the end of it ("Ten, nine, eight, seven"). You'd have to count mentally, or on your fingers, to the seventh piece of information. There's a better — infinitely better — way. And that way is the Peg System of memory.

The Peg System will enable you to memorize whatever you like in and out of order and by number. And there's a huge chunk of serendipity involved. (Serendipity: finding something great without extra effort.) *After* you learn to do just that — memorize items by number — the same information will enable you to do something *else* with your memory that nobody else could conceivably do!

The core of the Peg System (and the core of the systems I'll be teaching that enable you to remember numbers of any kind, no matter how and where they're used) is the Phonetic Number/ Alphabet. It's based on *sounds* and it is simple, fascinating, and *useful*.

There are ten digits in our numerical system: 1, 2, 3, 4, 5, 6, 7, 8, 9, 0. There are also, fortunately, only ten *basic* consonant sounds in our language. I know that technically there are more, but for our purposes, only the ten basic consonant sounds are important. It would seem that there are more than ten of those, but not so. That's because some letters make, basically, the same phonetic sound. For example, the letters T and D. They're different letters, but they make the same phonetic sound. One is "harder" than the other, that's all.

The rule is that when your vocal apparatus — lips, tongue, teeth — are in the same position when forming certain sounds, then those sounds are phonetically the same (at least for our purposes). When forming the T and D sound, the tip of your tongue hits the back of your upper front teeth. The D sound is softer, but they're phonetically the same.

If you understand that, the rest is easy. F (or PH) and V form the same phonetic sound. Your upper front teeth press against the inside of your lower lip for both of them. The V sound is softer than the F sound, but they're phonetically the same. P and B form the same phonetic sound; your lips purse the same way for each. K, hard G (as in green), and hard C (as in cake) are the same hard, back-of-the-throat, phonetic sound. J, SH, CH (as in cheese), and soft G (as in geology) all form the same phonetic sound, and so do Z, S, and soft C (as in center). They are the "hissing" sounds.

There are only ten of them. What I've done is to assign one of those sounds to each of the ten digits. Those pairs will always remain the same; so learn them and you'll use them for the rest of your life. They're easy to remember because you won't do it by rote memory. (I *eliminate* rote memory; I don't find uses for it!) I'll give you a quick memory aid for remembering each pair. You'll need that aid only at first. If you concentrate on the pairs and the silly little memory aids, you'll know them all after one reading.

Lock this in your mind: it is the *sounds* we're interested in — the sounds the letters make — not the letters themselves. You'll see why this is so in a moment. But also understand that I have to use the regular alphabet letters in order to teach the idea.

The digit 1 will always be represented by the sounds made by the letters **T** and **D**. **T** and **D** will always represent the number 1. The aid to help you remember that (you'll need it only now, to register it originally) is that the letter **T** has *one* downstroke. (Or, a **T** is formed with a digit 1 and a horizontal digit 1 lying on top.) Think of this for a moment.

The digit 2 will always be represented by the sound of the letter **N**. The lower-case typewritten letter **n** has *two* downstrokes. Think of that for a moment. (Think of each memory aid for a moment, so that I don't have to keep telling you to do so.)

The digit 3 is **M**. A typewritten small **m** has *three* downstrokes. Or, if you roll an **M** onto its side, it looks like a 3; put a 3 on its side, it looks like an **M**. One of our large corporations is the 3M Company.

The digit 4 is **R**. The word "fouR" ends with the **R** sound. Or, use a bit of imagination: Look at the **R**. Doesn't it look like a golfer about to tee off? And the word that's yelled when he tees off is "Fore!"

The digit 5 is **L**. The Roman numeral for 50 is **L**. Or, you can form the letter **L** with your 5 fingers, by holding your left hand palm outward, as if saying "stop." Stick the thumb straight out. An **L** is shaped.

The digit 6 is **J, SH,** soft **CH,** and soft **G** (as in gentle). A 6 and a capital **J** are almost mirror images. If you hold one up to the mirror it looks like the other: 6J.

The digit 7 is **K**, hard **C** (as in crazy), and hard **G** (as in great). You can form a capital **K** with two 7's; one right side up and the other almost upside down: K.

The digit 8 is **F, V,** and **PH** (as in philosophy). An 8 and a handwritten small letter **f** are similar in so far as each is formed with two loops, one above the other: 8f.

The digit 9 is **P** and **B**. The letter **P** and the digit 9 are almost exact mirror images: 9P.

The digit 0 is **S**, **Z**, and soft **C** (as in census). The first sound in the word "zero" is **Z**. (And the first sound in the word "cypher" is soft **C**.)

The only missing consonant sound is **TH** (as in "the"). This sound will rarely come up, but it will be the same as **T** and represent the digit 1. The vowels, **aeiou**, have no numerical value in my Phonetic Number/Alphabet. They will be our "wild cards," our "connectors," as you'll see. The letters **W**, **H**, and **Y** (*why*) have no numerical value. (The **H** does only when following other consonants which changes the sound.)

Silent letters have no numerical value because *they make no sound*. The word "knee" transposes to number 2, not 72. It's the sound that's important. In the word "knee," the **K** makes *no* sound, so it has no numerical value. The only consonant sound in that word is the **N** sound, and that sound represents, can represent only, the number 2.

The word "bomb" transposes to 93, not 939. The last **B** is silent, so it has no numerical value.

The same concept holds true for most double letters. The word "butter" transposes to 914 — not 9114. There are two **T**'s in the word, but those **T**'s form only one **T** sound. The word "pillow" transposes to 95; the double **L** makes a single **L** sound. This rule holds true for all double letters unless they each *do* make different sounds, as in "accident" (which transposes to 70121) or "vaccine" (8702).

The letter **Q** is pronounced like the letter **K**, so it represents 7. The letter **X** is never used, but it can be. It transposes according to the way it is sounded in a word. In the word "fix," the **X** would be written phonetically as **KS**, so it would transpose to 70. In the word "anxious," however, the **X** is pronounced "KSH," and it transposes to 76. So, to recap:

1 = **T, D** (a T has *one* downstroke)
2 = **N** (a small *n* has *two* downstrokes)
3 = **M** (a small *m* has *three* downstrokes)
4 = **R** (the word "fouR" ends with the R sound)

5 = L (the Roman numeral for 50 is L)
6 = J, SH, CH, soft G (a capital J is almost a mirror image of a 6: 6J)
7 = K, hard C, hard G (a capital K can be formed with a pair of 7's: 𝒦)
8 = F, V, PH (a handwritten small *f* and an 8 both have loops arranged one above the other: 8𝑓)
9 = P, B (a P and a 9 are almost exact mirror images: 9𝑃)
0 = S, Z, soft C (the word "Zero" begins with the Z sound)

Think of the little memory aid I gave you for each "pair" and you'll see that you already know most or all of them. You want to know them in and out of order, and I want them to be second nature to you. You can't possibly realize now how large a help they will be to you. Play this little practice game and you'll know them better than your ABCs: When you see a number — a license plate, an address, or whatever — mentally transpose the digits of that number to sounds. When you see a word on a billboard or any sign, mentally transpose the consonant sounds to digits.

I'll start you off with some drills. Go over the Phonetic Number/Alphabet one more time, then complete the drills; fill in all the blanks. Do that and you're well on your way to knowing the sounds perfectly. You'll be thrilled with the dividends this bit of practice will pay — I promise you that. The answers will follow so that you can check. Do not continue reading until you've completed the drills and feel that you know the Phonetic Number/Alphabet.

Drills: Phonetic Number/Alphabet

P = __9__   R = ____   hard C (cat) = ____   L = ____

B = ____   hard G (go) = ____   K = ____   N = ____

D = ____   V = ____   J = ____   soft C (cigar) = ____

M = ____   T = ____   Z = ____   S = ____   CH = ____

4 = __R__   1 = ____   0 = ____   8 = ____

9 = ____   5 = ____   2 = ____   6 = ____

7 = ____   3 = ____

729 = __KNP__   436 = ____   381 = ____   529 = ____

123 = ____   890 = ____   567 = ____   345 = ____

089 = ____   553 = ____   778 = ____   787 = ____

877 = ____   004 = ____   400 = ____   040 = ____

912 = ____   023 = ____   333 = ____   667 - ____

6215 = __JNTL__   53091 = ____   26 = ____

935210 = ____   481623 = ____   24680 = ____

97531 = ____   08 = ____   231560 = ____

0011223 = ____   911998 = ____   128145 = ____

patter = __914__   butter = ____   biter = ____

tub = ____   bidder = ____   bite rye = ____

terror = ____   break = ____   vision = ____

chandelier = ____   telephone = ____   pillow = ____

bookkeeper = ____   bringing = ____   mellow = ____

packaging = ____   porcelain = ____   scissors = ____

Mississippi = ____   Philadelphia = ____   big deal = ____

tattle = ____   tailors = ____   carefully = ____

Drill Answers Check these answers against yours. If any do not match, go back and find out *why*.

P = 9	R = 4	hard C = 7	L = 5
B = 9	hard G = 7	K = 7	N = 2
D = 1	V = 8	J = 6	soft C = 0
M = 3	T = 1	Z = 0	S = 0 CH = 6

4 = R	1 = T, D	0 = S, Z, soft C	8 = F, V, PH
9 = P, B	5 = L	2 = N	6 = J, SH,
7 = K, hard C,	3 = M		CH, soft G
hard G			

729 = KNP	436 = RMJ	381 = MFT	529 = LNP
123 = TNM	890 = FPS	567 = LJK	345 = MRL
089 = SFP	553 = LLM	778 = KKF	787 = KFK
877 = FKK	004 = SSR	400 = RSS	040 = SRS
912 = PTN	823 = FNM	333 = MMM	667 = JJK

6215 = JNTL	53091 = LMSPT	26 = NJ
935210 = PMLNTS	481623 = RFTJNM	24680 = NRJFS
97531 = PKLMT	08 = SF	231560 = NMTLJS
0011223 = SSTTNNM	911998 = PTTPPF	128145 = TNFTRL

patter = 914	butter = 914	biter = 914
tub = 19	bidder = 914	bite rye = 914
terror = 144	break = 947	vision = 862
chandelier = 62154	telephone = 1582	pillow = 95
bookkeeper = 9794	bringing = 942727	mellow = 35
packaging = 97627	porcelain = 94052	scissors = 0040
Mississippi = 3009	Philadelphia = 85158	big deal = 9715
tattle = 115	tailors = 1540	carefully = 7485

Chapter 7

Numbers and More

• • •

Amaze Yourself

*T*ry to hang your jacket on the blackboard and it will fall to the floor. Affix a short peg to that blackboard, and you can hang up the jacket easily. I want to give you some pegs — no, not for your blackboard, but to affix within your mind. Once you do that, you'll be able to "hang" *any* information onto those pegs, which is why I call this the *Peg* System of memory. And you'll be able to use those Pegs over and over and over again — forever.

If you know the sounds of the Phonetic Number/Alphabet, you can come up with a word that will represent any number. Ordinarily, numbers are the most difficult things to remember because they're nothing but designs, concepts; they can't be visualized. (What does 7 mean to you and me except that it's one higher than 6 and one lower than 8?)

Now, however, knowing the sounds of the Phonetic Number/ Alphabet will enable you to picture numbers. If you wanted to remember the number 17, all you'd need is a word (picture) that would represent *only* that number. The word "tack," for instance. The **T** sound is 1 and the **K** sound (**ck**) is 7. Just the **T** and **K** sounds would be as difficult to remember as 17, but that's where the vowels come in. The **a** makes it easy to form a *word* containing only those two sounds (in the correct order) and that word can be seen in your mind's eye! A tack can be pictured — and "tack," in the Phonetic Number/Alphabet, can represent *only* 17. Visualizing a tack, therefore, *is the same as visualizing the number 17.*

You can make *any* number meaningful by using the sounds you've learned. If you pictured a *big truck,* you'd be "seeing"

97147. *Broken lamp* would *tell* you . . . 9472539. You can make up words as the need arises, but it's much better, it saves time, to have some words ready to work for you. These are called Peg Words, and *tack* is the Peg Word for 17. I'll teach you the first ten Pegs, which you'll know after the first reading. Then, you'll learn a fascinating way to use those Pegs.

The word for number 1 must contain only *one* consonant sound, because 1 is a *single* digit, and that one sound must be **T** or **D** because that's the sound that represents (transposes to) 1. There are many words that would do. I've selected *tie*. *Tie* can represent *only* the number 1, and it is easy to picture. So, the Peg Word for 1 will *always* be *tie*.

The Peg Word for 2 also must contain only one consonant sound, but that sound has to be **N**. I've selected the word (name) *Noah*. You can picture the ark, animals, or, as I do, an old man with a long, gray beard (or just the beard). The Peg Word for 2 will always be *Noah*.

The Peg Word for 3 is *ma* because it contains only the **M** sound. Picture your mother (or any mother) for *ma*.

The Peg Word for 4 is *rye*. Picture a loaf of rye bread or a bottle of rye whiskey.

For number 5, I use the Peg Word *law*. Picture a policeman, who represents the law.

Number 6 is *shoe*. There are no choices to make: *shoe* can represent *only* the number 6. Picture a shoe, of course.

Number 7 is *cow*. Picture the bovine animal.

Number 8 is *ivy*. The **V** sound represents 8. Picture the ivy that grows on college walls.

Number 9 is *bee*. Picture the stinging insect.

The number 10 has *two* digits, therefore its Peg Word must contain two consonant sounds, the **T** and **S**, *in that order*. I've selected *toes*. The sounds *tell* you what number the word represents. *Toes* could represent only number 10.

If I gave you ten words arbitrarily, the system would still work, but you'd have to use rote memory to remember the words. That is not the case here. Because you know the sounds, knowing the words is hardly a memory problem at all. I gave you a memory aid to help you remember the sounds themselves; now those sounds help to remember the Peg Words. (Then the Peg Words will help you remember other information.) Go over the first ten Peg Words once more.

1. **Tie**		6. **SHoe**	
2. **Noah**		7. **Cow**	
3. **Ma**		8. **iVy**	
4. **Rye**		9. **Bee**	
5. **Law**		10. **ToeS**	

Look away from this page and see if you know them all. And, because you know the sounds out of order, you'll also know the Peg Words out of order. Before you continue, make sure you're familiar with these first ten. Fill in the following blanks.

4 = ____   8 = ____   6 = ____   3 = ____   10 = ____

5 = ____   2 = ____   7 = ____   9 = ____   1 = ____

BEE = ____   NOAH = ____   RYE = ____   TIE = ____

TOES = ____   SHOE = ____   LAW = ____   IVY = ____

MA = ____   COW = ____

Now that you know them, what good do these Peg Words do you? Well, remember that I asked you how you'd know the seventh mineral in the hardness scale? You had to count to it in your Link. But if you associate (just as you've already learned) *quartz* to *cow*, you'll know that quartz is the seventh mineral *instantly!* Form your silly, ridiculous, or impossible picture between *quarter* (or *quarts* or *warts* — whatever you're using to *remind* you of quartz) and *cow*. That's all. You can "see" yourself milking a cow, and millions of quarters come out instead of milk, or millions of quarts come out (visualizing millions makes it silly). See that picture, because we'll go through the rest of the hardness scale as the teaching example (and we'll do it *out of sequence* just to prove a point).

The fourth mineral is fluorite. Associate *floor right* to *rye*.

Perhaps, a floor is drinking from a large bottle of rye and saying "right." Or, your floor (which is really enough to remind you of fluorite) is a gigantic loaf of rye bread. Be sure to see the picture you've selected or made up.

The first mineral is talc. I remembered it by seeing myself pouring *talc*um powder all over my expensive *tie*. You may want to see a gigantic *tie talk*ing. Most important: see the picture.

Number 9 is corumdum. A *bee* is stinging a gigantic apple core; the core is acting *dumb*. You can see it drinking rum, if you think it's necessary. Or, a dumb bee is drinking rum. See the picture you think will remind you of the two vital pieces of information — the number and the mineral.

Number 2 is gypsum. See *Noah* (old man with beard) dressed as a *gypsy*; or see a gypsy hanging from a man's chin — the gypsy *is* the beard. Or, Noah is *chipping some* wood from the ark. See the picture.

Number 10 is diamond. Just see lots of *diamonds* between your *toes*. Or, your toes *are* diamonds. Do see the picture.

Number 3 is calcite. Visualize your *ma* sitting on a *cold site*, or she's calling to a height (*calls height*). See the one you select or make up yourself.

Number 8 is topaz. See *ivy* growing all over a *dopey ass*, or ivy is trying *to pass* you. See the picture.

Number 6 is feldspar. You might see a gigantic *shoe* having been *felled* while *spar*ring. Be sure to see the picture.

And, finally, number 5 is opalite. Picture a policeman (*law*) being *oh* so *polite*, or making an *opal light*. *See* the picture you select in your mind's eye.

Did you really try to *see* all the pictures? If not, go back and do that now. If you did — again, get ready to amaze yourself. I made you "take" the information in a haphazard order, but your mind is the best computer of all. It has put that information *in order for you*. Prove it to yourself right now. Think of your Peg Words from 1 to 10, that's all. Each Peg will *tell* you the mineral for that number! Let's do it this way: Since this is the first time you've tried it, in the first column, I'll give you the Peg Words. Fill in the blanks of that column first. Then, cover that column with a piece of paper or your hand and fill in the blanks of the second column. Do that now. (Fill in the blanks as quickly as you can.)

1 (tie) = _____	1 = _____
2 (Noah) = _____	2 = _____
3 (ma) = _____	3 = _____
4 (rye) = _____	4 = _____
5 (law) = _____	5 = _____
6 (shoe) = _____	6 = _____
7 (cow) = _____	7 = _____
8 (ivy) = _____	8 = _____
9 (bee) = _____	9 = _____
10 (toes) = _____	10 = _____

You should be feeling quite good about yourself. But so far, you haven't really done anything so very different than what you did when you applied the Link System. You know the ten items in order (the only difference is that I gave them to you out of order). You can do something different right now — because if you know your Peg Words, you know the minerals out of order; that means that you know the *position* of each mineral. And the better you know your Peg Words (remember, you've just learned them), the faster you'll know those positions. What is the sixth mineral in the hardness scale? Just think of *shoe*. What was the shoe doing? It was felled, and so forth. That will immediately remind you of . . . feldspar. It's that simple. See how quickly you can fill in these blanks:

2 is _____   10 is _____

5 is _____   7 is _____

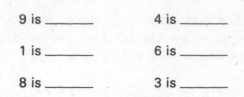

9 is _____   4 is _____

1 is _____   6 is _____

8 is _____   3 is _____

If you hear or read the *mineral*, you'll know its position! At what number in the scale is topaz? What does *dopey ass* or *to pass* remind you of? Ivy, of course. And *ivy* is your Peg Word for 8. So, topaz is the eighth mineral in the scale! Fill in these blanks, quickly.

feldspar is # _____   calcite is # _____

corumdum is # _____   talc is # _____

diamond is # _____   topaz is # _____

gypsum is # _____   opalite is # _____

quartz is # _____   fluorite is # _____

You now know the minerals by number — forward, backward, inside out! You know them as well as you can *possibly* know them. Test yourself any way you like, and you'll see that it is so.

You can do the same thing with any list, of course. Take a breather, then apply the Peg Word idea to the following list (it might be a list your friend has called off to you):

#8 is wristwatch   #4 is briefcase
#1 is pen   #10 is knife
#6 is cup   #2 is television set
#9 is stapler   #7 is rope
#5 is flower   #3 is carpet

If you've memorized these ten things in and out of order, by number — if you've tested yourself, and really know them — then you understand the Peg Word idea. Now, what do you do if you have to memorize 11 items, or 24, or 58? Isn't it obvious? You need Peg Words for all those numbers. You can make up the words as needed, but it's best just to have them ready. I'll give you the Peg Words up to 100. It's so easy, because you already know the sounds. If you wanted to make up a word for 72, you'd simply think of the proper sounds: **K** and **N**. Say them to yourself — **K** . . . **N**. And you'll probably come up with *coin*, which is the Peg Word for 72. The Peg Word for 11 must have a **T** (or **D**) and another **T** (or **D**) sound. The word is *tot*. For 12, you need a **T, N**; *tin* (picture anything you need to remember at number 12 made out of tin). The word I've selected for 13 is *tomb*. Don't let the **b** throw you; it's silent. Picture a gravestone.

Learn ten at a time and before you know it, you'll know them all. Do learn at least the first twenty. Then you'll be able to memorize twenty things by number. All the words are easy to picture, and after a while, you won't even think of the sounds; the picture you've selected will come right to mind.

1. tie	26. notch	51. lot	76. cage
2. Noah	27. neck	52. lion	77. coke
3. ma	28. knife	53. limb	78. cave
4. rye	29. knob	54. lure	79. cob
5. law	30. mouse	55. lily	80. fez
6. shoe	31. mat	56. leech	81. fat
7. cow	32. moon	57. log	82. phone
8. ivy	33. mummy	58. lava	83. foam
9. bee	34. mower	59. lip	84. fur
10. toes	35. mule	60. cheese	85. file
11. tot	36. match	61. sheet	86. fish
12. tin	37. mug	62. chain	87. fog
13. tomb	38. movie	63. jam	88. fife
14. tire	39. mop	64. cherry	89. fob (or fib)
15. towel	40. rose	65. jail	90. bus
16. dish	41. rod	66. choo-choo	91. bat
17. tack	42. rain	67. chalk	92. bone
18. dove	43. ram	68. chef	93. bum
19. tub	44. rower	69. ship	94. bear
20. nose	45. roll	70. case	95. bell
21. net	46. roach	71. cot	96. beach
22. nun	47. rock	72. coin	97. book
23. name	48. roof	73. comb	98. puff
24. Nero	49. rope	74. car	99. pipe
25. nail	50. lace	75. coal	100. disease (or dozes, teases, thesis)

I'll answer some of your questions soon; right now, here's a drill on the 100 Peg Words. Try to fill in all the blanks correctly without looking back and you will *know* the words.

65 = jail	bear = ____	35 = ____	neck = ____
96 = ____	tack = ____	66 = ____	lot = ____
8 = ____	lure = ____	foam = ____	36 = ____
49 = ____	mummy = ____	tire = ____	91 = ____
42 = ____	86 = ____	pipe = ____	tin = ____
rye = ____	1 = ____	46 = ____	23 = ____
100 = ____	bus = ____	moon = ____	bell = ____
nose = ____	85 = ____	leech = ____	67 = ____
2 = ____	89 = ____	cob = ____	notch = ____
limb = ____	mouse = ____	92 = ____	31 = ____
16 = ____	21 = ____	fife = ____	rower = ____
sheet = ____	cave = ____	55 = ____	coke = ____
93 = ____	15 = ____	lava = ____	37 = ____
5 = ____	10 = ____	75 = ____	puff = ____
73 = ____	52 = ____	6 = ____	mop = ____
jam = ____	94 = ____	ma = ____	knife = ____
65 = ____	59 = ____	97 = ____	7 = ____
40 = ____	fez = ____	69 = ____	72 = ____
ram = ____	19 = ____	nail = ____	cherry = ____

76 = ___	38 = ___	9 = ___	fat = ___
68 = ___	74 = ___	34 = ___	roof = ___
fog = ___	84 = ___	57 = ___	11 = ___
22 = ___	phone = ___	60 = ___	24 = ___
roll = ___	62 = ___	dove = ___	rod = ___
29 = ___	71 = ___	13 = ___	70 = ___
	47 = ___	50 = ___	

When you want to remember numbers with more than two digits — say, three or four — you can simply associate two Peg Words to remind you of them. For example, to remember the date 1820, you might visualize a *dove* (18) on your *nose* (20). But it isn't necessary to use Peg Words for numbers with more than two digits. Use your imagination and think of a word (**divans**) or phrase (**tough knees**) that fits. Remember that a phrase, two or more words, is still usually only one picture in your mind. Why not try it now? Try to come up with three or four words or phrases for each of the following. Then compare yours to mine.

8270 _____

3624 _____

2120 _____

4215 _____

7214 _____

8270: fangs; fungus; fine kiss; ivy nicks; fine keys; view necks; vine gas

3624: machinery; matchin' ore; mission rye; my shiner; mush in hair; ma join her; imaginary

2120: Indians; knot nose; end noose; no dunce; new dance; hen dunes; intense
4215: ruined all; rental; iron tail; ear nettle; ran doll; rained eel; runt hill; errand owl
7214: cantor; counter; keynoter; gained hair; kinder; candor; again tore; gowned her

With a bit of imagination, *anything* can be pictured. It can be an action or a situation. You might look at 7321 and come up with *command* (*comment* would do, too). Can you picture command? Sure. You might imagine an officer commanding troops. Picture whatever makes *you* think of the word. (Yes — *commando* is perfect.)

Bonus: I don't think it's too important for you to remember *long* numbers for schoolwork. Then again, who knows? It may be something that will come in handy. The point is that you can already do it: there's nothing new for you to learn! You need to know the Link System and the Phonetic Number/Alphabet, and you already know them. Look . . .

94836395390942727

Form a Link: **perfume** (9483) to **jump** (639) to **lamps** (5390) to **brain** (942) to **king** (727) — or to **bringing** (942727). Form the Link (four pictures!) and you'll know that number forward and backward! **Brave** to **my chum** to **plump** to **sprain** to **kinky** would also do.

Link my examples *big truck* and *broken lamp* (a big truck is carrying a gigantic broken lamp, perhaps) and you've memorized 971479472539. See that broken lamp as it is lighting up an entire **skyscraper** and you'll know 9714794725390707494. And if that lit-up skyscraper is somehow acting as your **dentist**, you'll know 971479472539070749412101 — a *24-digit* number — by forming a four-picture Link!

Questions and Answers

Q. Why is the Phonetic Number/Alphabet based on sounds and not the letters of the alphabet?

A. Because based on sounds, the system works even for a person who can't read or speak well. Also, many letters make different sounds in different words. (One way to spell "fish" is **ghoti: gh** as in cou**gh**, **o** as in w**o**men, and **ti** as in na**ti**on.) Using the letters would complicate what is now a simple idea.

Q. Can I use the Peg Words to remember more than one list?

A. Of course. Once you've used the Pegs to memorize one list of information, it's like a magic slate; it becomes available again. And keep in mind that once you've locked any information into your memory, the original associations fade; the information remains.

Q. Should I Link the Peg Words to help me remember them?

A. No. Don't create problems where none exist. The sounds are the only aids you'll need. And if you should have trouble thinking of a Peg Word at first, simply add vowel sounds after or between the consonant sounds and the word will come to mind. For example, suppose you're not sure which is the Peg Word for 51, but you know that the sounds are **L** and **T**. Say to yourself, "Lat, late, let, leet, lit, light, loot, *lot*." The instant you think "lot," you'll know that *that's* the correct Peg Word.

Q. Why can't I simply Link Peg Words in order to memorize a long number?

A. You can, but why would you want to? Why use three Peg Words to remember the number 621540 when one word (**chandeliers**) would do it? No. Throw in a Peg Word if you're stuck but, basically, use the Peg Words to help you remember things by number.

Q. When using the Peg System, must my pictures be silly or ridiculous?

A. Always try to make the pictures ridiculous. That's what forces Original Awareness, that's what makes the system *work*. Before you know it, the silly, ridiculous picture will come to mind before a logical one does.

Q. What should I do if more than one silly picture runs through my mind for one association?

A. Don't worry about it. Just see one of them clearly.

Q. Can I make up Peg Words for numbers higher than 100?

A. Of course you can. For 101, *test, toast, dust;* for 102, *dozen, dozin'* or *Edison;* 103 — *toss me, toss 'em;* 104 — *teaser, dicer;* 105 — *tassle, tussle, docile;* 106 — *dosage;* 107 — *task, tusk, dusk.* There's no limit: 314, *motor;* 926, *bench.* But you really don't need to make up "high" Peg Words in advance. That may defeat the purpose. It's just as easy and maybe faster to make them up as you need them. That way, you're not tying yourself into a specific word. It's up to you.

Chapter 8

Vocabulary

• • •

*You __Can__ Remember Words
and Definitions Easily*

All three basic ideas or systems taught in this book (Link, Peg, Substitute Word) are extremely important and useful. But it's the Substitute Word idea that enables the other two to work as well as they do. That's because it helps you to visualize intangible information, the kind that cannot ordinarily be pictured in the mind, the kind that's ordinarily the most difficult to remember.

It's interesting, challenging, and easy to learn names — of people, places, and things — when you apply the Substitute Word System of memory. That same technique makes it easy and interesting to remember any technical terminology and foreign- and English-language vocabulary!

Sounds great, doesn't it? It is — and you've already applied it, so you *already* know the basic idea. I eased you into the technique when I taught you to memorize the hardness scale with the Link and with the Peg. The mineral names would ordinarily not be easy to visualize, and therefore not easy to memorize. I taught you to think up a word or phrase for each one that *sounds like* the name — enough so that it would *remind* you of it — and that *can* be visualized or pictured. For "gypsum," *gypsy* or *chip some*; for "topaz," *toe pass* or *dope ass*; and so forth.

That's it — that's basically the Substitute Word System of memory. The sound-alike word or phrase you select enables you to visualize the conglomeration of sound that you'd ordinarily not be able to visualize. I did the same thing for you where numbers are concerned. The Phonetic Number/Alphabet enables you to *visualize* numbers.

To "lock in" the Substitute Word idea: Assume you never heard the word "barbecue" before and you wanted to remember not only its pronunciation but also its meaning. What does "barbecue" sound like? *Barber Q* (or *cue*), of course.

Now, that picture, which will remind you of the pronunciation, must be connected (associated) to the *meaning* of the word.

Seeing a silly picture of a barber working on a gigantic letter **Q** or on a cue stick as that **Q** or cue stick roasts on an open grill would do it. That association would remind you of both the pronunciation of the word and its meaning: one would remind you of the other! Think of open grill and *barber cue* comes to mind; think of barber cue and *open grill* comes to mind. You can't lose!

To plagiarize is to steal someone else's ideas. See this silly picture in your mind: You've come up with this great idea of playing with your eyes (*played your eyes* — plagiarize). Really see that ridiculous picture of playing with your eyes. Then visualize everyone else doing the same thing: they've *stolen your idea.*

Silly? You bet. Does it work? You bet! "Silly" is the *point.* Try this one: A *sycophant* is a flatterer who seeks favors, a servile person. Imagine an *ant* (or *aunt*) continually trying to win your favor by flattering you, being overly servile, to the point that it makes you *sick*. You're *sick of ant*.

If you really want to remember (learn, know) certain words, applying this technique will force you to concentrate on pronunciation and definition for at least a second or so; it will force Original Awareness — no way to avoid that. The association itself — the silly picture — will "lock" the information into your memory. After that, when you read, hear, think the word, the definition will come to mind. When you think the definition, the word will instantly come to mind. It works better than you can possibly imagine right now.

To really "set" the technique for you, I'll show you how to apply it to foreign-language vocabulary. I will come back to English vocabulary immediately after. That's very important, particularly if you're approaching the SAT time of scholastic life. And most of my examples will be words most often tested on the SAT exams! (*Sycophant* is one of them.) But first, let's practice a bit by learning how to apply the technique to foreign words.

Chapter 9

Foreign-Language Vocabulary

• • •

Très Facile

*A*pplying the Substitute Word technique to foreign-language words or phrases is practical and serves as practice toward applying it to English words as well. And applying it to English words is obviously practical but also excellent practice toward applying it to the terminology and the work of just about every other school subject. The systems are self-perpetuating: the more you use them, the more use you'll find for them and the more useful they'll be.

And — quite important — all my methods are *means to an end*. Once you reach the "end," which is the learning of a new piece of information, the "means" (the silly pictures, associations) are no longer needed. View the systems as the streets that connect the *encountering* of that information to the *knowing* of that information. That's precisely why you don't have to worry about those ridiculous pictures running around in your mind forever. *Trying* to apply the systems *forces* Original Awareness — and *that's* the key to remembering, the key to *learning*. The systems bring you to the end (you've *learned*); then you can "forget" the means! Let's prove that some more.

Through the years, students have told me that one of the most fascinating and useful applications of the Substitute Word technique is employing it to master foreign-language vocabulary. Once you understand the idea (you already do!), you can *learn* twenty, thirty, or more foreign words and their English meanings every day. The Substitute Word System enables you to memorize them quickly and easily, and *retain* them for as long as you want to — *forever*, if you like.

For example, and for practice, consider the Swedish word for men's trousers: *bygsor*. It's pronounced "beeg-sore." All you have to do is associate *big sore*, *beak sore*, or *big saw* (you've just made the meaningless conglomeration of sound meaningful) to trousers. You might "see" a gigantic pair of pants (no one in them, just the pants) with a *big sore* on them. Or, a bird is pecking on a pair of pants until its *beak* is *sore*. Really see one of those pictures, because I'll be testing you on this and the following examples; I want you to see, definitely, how well it works.

Consider these Portuguese words: The word for *purse* is *bolsa*. Visualize a gigantic purse made of *balsa* wood, or full of balsa. See it. *Jantar* means *dinner* in Portuguese. Can you visualize a *john* (or a friend named John, or a *janitor*) eating *tar* (*john tar*) for *dinner*? Then do so now. *Saia* ("sy-er") is a *skirt*. See a skirt sighing; it's a *sigher*. The word *peùgas* ("pee-oo-gesh"; the "sh" is a soft sound as in "Asia") means *socks*. A suggestion: visualize a gigantic sock having an awful odor; you say to it, "*Peeyoo*, you smell like *gas*." *See* these pictures.

Even if both the foreign word *and* its English equivalent are not definite, concrete pictures in your mind, you can still apply the system because the Substitute Word technique makes them both meaningful. The Thai word for the month of August is *Singhakom*. A *gust* of wind will remind you of Au*gust*. See a gigantic comb singing (singing comb, or a comb is singing and laughing — *sing ha comb*) and a gust of wind blows it away. It's silly, but see the picture and you'll *know* the word and its meaning! The Greek word for *scissors* is transliterated as *psalidi* (the "p" is pronounced). A pair of scissors is passing a lady (*pass a lady*). See that picture.

I've just given you seven new foreign words and their meanings. If you've *tried* to make the associations (if you haven't, go back and make them now), you *know* them — there's no doubt about it. See for yourself. Turn the page and fill in the blanks.

Saia means _____ in Portuguese. *Singhakom* means _____ in Thai. *Bygsor* means _____ in Swedish. *Psalidi* means _____ in Greek. And in Portuguese, *peùgas* means _____, *bolsa* means _____, and *jantar* is _____.

Did you know all or most of them? Good. Try this now (and don't worry about spelling).

The word for *socks* in Portuguese is _____. *Purse* in Portuguese is _____; *August* (Thai) is _____; *scissors* (Greek) is _____; *trousers* (Swedish) is _____; *dinner* and *skirt* (Portuguese) are _____ and _____.

Try a few more. The Spanish word *hermano* ("air-mon-o") means *brother*. *Airman* would be a good Substitute Word. Form a ridiculous picture of *brother* and *airman*. Your brother — and if you don't have a brother, picture a fellow who looks like you — is an airman. Perhaps he's flying a large letter *O* instead of a plane. *Airman O — hermano*. See the picture.

Ventana means *window* in Spanish. See a girl named *Anna* throwing a *vent* (air conditioner) through a closed *window*. *Vent Anna — ventana*. See it in your mind's eye.

Mariposa is the Spanish word for *butterfly*. Picture a girl named *Mary posing* while a gigantic butterfly lands on her head. You can use *marry* instead of *Mary*. You might see a gigantic butterfly posing as it's being married. See it.

Desperador is the Spanish word for *alarm clock*. *Desperate door* or *this pair o' doors* would do as Substitute Words or phrases, as would *this pear a door*. Associate alarm clock to one of those. You might picture a gigantic alarm clock being a *door*, and it's *desperate* to get away. See (and hear) the alarm clock ringing to get action into your picture.

Estrella ("eh-stray-a") is the Spanish word for *star*. You could picture a gigantic letter *S straying* — the *S* is a *strayer* — all the way to a star. Even *S spraying a* star would be enough to remind you. See the picture.

Pantufla is the Spanish word for *slipper*. See a gigantic *pan* trying *to fly;* or *two pans* are about to *fly*.

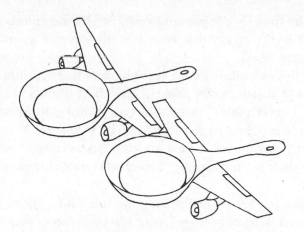

Pan to fly or *pan two fly* — *pantufla*. Associate slipper to either one; perhaps you're wearing pans instead of slippers, and the pans are about to fly. See it.

Again, if you've seen these few pictures in your mind's eye, you should have no trouble filling in these blanks.

mariposa means _____	*estrella* means _____
hermano means _____	*pantufla* means _____
ventana means _____	*desperador* means _____

A few French words: *Bouchon* means *cork*. *Push on* or *bush on* would do it. See yourself *push*ing *on* a gigantic cork, or a *bush* is growing *on* a gigantic cork, or you're saying *boo* to a gigantic cork because it *shone* a light on you.

In France, a *grapefruit* is a *pamplemousse*. Seems difficult, but it isn't at all. Just see a *moose* covered with large *pimples* and those pimples are all really *grapefruits*. That's all you have to do — see it.

Talon is the French word for *heel*. The English word *talon* means a claw. So you can see a gigantic claw growing out of your heel, or something growing *tall on* your heel. Either will do. I'm not specifically into pronunciation here. If you're studying a particular language you *know* how certain letters and certain words, in that language, are pronounced. I'm interested in teaching you how to give yourself *reminders*.

The French word for *squirrel* is *écureuil*. *Egg cure oil* is close to that conglomeration of sound, close enough to remind you of it (even though the final *l* is not pronounced). See the ridiculous picture of a squirrel laying an *egg* that runs toward some *oil* in order to *cure* it — *egg cure oil*.

Apply the Substitute Word technique to foreign phrases in the same way. *S'il vous plaît* is *please* in French. It sounds like "seal boo play" or "silver plate." Associate one of those to *please*. (You're saying "please" to a large *silver plate*, or vice versa.)

C'est trop cher means *it's too expensive*. Associate *sit row chair* or *say throw share* to the meaning. Select your own silly picture — and see it.

Il me faut (*eel my foe* could be your substitute phrase) means *I need*. An eel is coming to get you; it's your foe — you *need* help, and yell for it, "*I need* help!"

L'addition is the *check* for a meal. It sounds like *lad dish yawn*. A lad is looking at a dish and yawning as he pays the check.

I've asked you to see the pictures for four French words and four French phrases. Now test yourself.

c'est trop cher means _____	*talon* means _____
pamplemousse means _____	*s'il vous plaît* means _____
l'addition means _____	*écureuil* means _____
bouchon means _____	*il me faut* means _____

If you've made the pictures and filled in the blanks, then I've proven the point. More important, you've proven the point to yourself. And if you need help remembering the articles (feminine or masculine) in any language, make up a word that will represent one of them all the time. The masculine article in Spanish is *el;* feminine is *la.* It's easy in Spanish because most feminine *nouns* end with an *a.* Anyway, a word to represent masculine could be *el,* the abbreviation for elevated train. Stick an el train into your picture for a masculine noun, that's all. When you think that picture again, you'll "see" the el train and know it's masculine. If there's no el in your picture, it's a feminine noun.

In French, the articles are *le* (masculine) and *la* (feminine). Same technique. You might decide to picture *la* (singing la, la, la) as your standard picture for the feminine article. See one of the items in any picture for a feminine noun *singing.* If nothing in your picture is singing, the noun is masculine.

Another way, for any language: Get a *dress* into your picture for any feminine noun. If there's no dress in it, it's masculine.

Would you like a bit more practice on applying the Substitute Word technique to foreign-language vocabulary? Okay. Below are six Spanish words (they're pronounced as spelled) and six French words (I'll give you the approximate pronunciations). Come up with your own Substitute Word or phrase for each one, and associate that to the English meaning. In other words, *learn* the following words. Test yourself to see if you really know them after applying the system. Then, if you want to, you can compare your Substitute Words with mine.

SPANISH	FRENCH
corbata — necktie	*échelle* (ay-shell) — ladder
correr — to run	*cicatrice* (see-ka-treess) — scar
pelota — ball	*manche* (mawnsh) — sleeve
preguntar — to ask	*escargot* (ess-car-go) — snail
cantar — to sing	*pomme* (pumm) — apple
cuadro — picture	*ongle* (awngl) — fingernail

After you've tested yourself, you can check below to see how I might learn these words.

Corbata — necktie. There's a large apple *core* around my neck instead of a *necktie* and I'm hitting it with a *bat.*

Correr — to run. Someone is coring gigantic pieces of fruit (he's a *corer*) and *running* as he does it. (*Core air* would also do.)

Pelota — ball. A *pail o' tar* is playing *ball*.

Preguntar — to ask. I'm *praying* to a *gun* that's covered with sticky *tar* and *asking* it questions.

Cantar — to sing. I'm *tearing* a tin *can* because it's *singing* too loudly. (Or, I'm *tarring* the can.)

Cuadro — picture. A *squad* is *rowing* a gigantic *picture* instead of a rowboat.

Échelle — ladder. A *shell* is climbing a *ladder*. Or, a large letter *A* is carrying a *shell* and climbing a *ladder*.

Cicatrice — scar. I *see* a gigantic *car* among the *trees*, crashing into them and causing *scars*. Or a large letter *C* is *cutting rice* (C *cut rice*) and causing *scars*.

Manche — sleeve. I see myself *munch*ing on a gigantic *sleeve*.

(If I picture it as the sleeve of a *dress*, I know that it's feminine.) Or, a gigantic *sleeve* is *munch*ing on me.

Escargot — snail. A gigantic *snail* is shaped like the letter *S*; it gets into a *car* and makes it *go*.

Pomme — apple. I visualize a gigantic *apple* with *pom*-poms all over it; or I could see myself *pummeling* an *apple*.

Ongle — fingernail. A gigantic *fingernail* is my *uncle*. Or, my *fingernail* is very large and it's bent up at an *angle*.

The length of a word is immaterial. A Greek man told me that the longest word in the Greek language is the word for "worm and ant hole." He transliterated it as *skoulikomermigotripa*. I broke it down, phonetically, like this: *school, lea, core, mermaid, got ripper.* Link those concepts to the meaning of the word and you'll "have" it. I pictured *ant holes* attending *school;* the school is in a *lea* (meadow); the lea is covered with apple *cores;* a *mermaid* is eating the cores; someone comes to rip the mermaid, but she *got* the *ripper.* I used *core* instead of *go* because that's closer to the actual pronunciation; a crow's *caw* would also do. Instead of *got ripper,* you could use *got rip Pa* or *go trip her;* instead of *mermaid,* you could use *murmur.* Whatever you think of is fine. You'll hesitate when saying the word at first, but not after the third or fourth time, I assure you.

When studying French, one major memory problem is that of knowing the 16 common nonreflexive verbs that are conjugated with *être* rather than *avoir.* Here they are:

descendre — to go down	*venir* — to come
devenir — to become	*rentrer* — to come back; reenter
entrer — to enter	*retourner* — to return; revisit
partir — to leave	*tomber* — to fall
aller — to go	*mourir* — to die
arriver — to arrive	*monter* — to go up; climb
rester — to remain; stay	*naître* — to be born
revenir — to come back (again)	*sortir* — to go out; leave

A teacher I know tells her students to think of the word *departments* because those letters can act as a memory aid. Another professor tells his students to think of a house, because most of the actions could take place in one. You are *born* in a house and *die* in a house; you *return* to a house and *enter* and *leave* a house, and so forth.

Neither of these techniques is definite enough. If we assume that you know the meanings of the words and that being reminded of them is tantamount to knowing the French words, then a simple Link will do it for you. The "house" idea is fine. Start the Link with a Substitute Word or phrase that will remind you of *être* — *eat raw,* for example. I learned the words using the following

Link. It's almost logical, so make each picture as ridiculous as you can. The basic idea:

You're *eating* a large piece of *raw* meat as you *come* (*venir*) to a gigantic house; you *enter* (*entrer*) and *go down* (descendre) a flight of stairs in order to get some more raw meat; you *fall down* (*tomber*) the stairs; then *climb up* (*monter*) again and *leave* (*partir*) the house; someone shouts, *"Come back again"* (*revenir*), so you *reenter* (*rentrer*); you *go* (*aller*) to the staircase again as someone *arrives* (*arriver*) and *becomes* (*devenir*) very angry; you are frightened and know that if you *remain* (*rester*), you will *die* (*mourir*), so you *go out* (*sortir*) into the fresh air and feel as if you've been *born* (*naître*) again; you vow that you'll never *return* (*retourner*) to that house.

Go over this Link a few times (that is, really see the pictures) and you'll know the verbs. There are some slight shades of difference in some of the meanings as I've used the words; that's not important here. We're assuming that you know the exact meanings — it's the reminder that's important. If you like, you can see the raw meat in a *dish* (Peg Word for 16) to remind you that there are 16 of the verbs.

If you'd rather, you can form a Link of the Substitute Words for the French words. That shouldn't be necessary, because you probably won't be faced with this problem until you already know the French words and their meanings. As you continue to learn how to apply my systems, you'll find different ways to handle this particular kind of problem. What I've just taught you, however, will do nicely.

I'll be answering some questions about the Substitute Word System at the end of chapter 10. In the meantime, you should go back and check to see if you know *all* the foreign words I've used as examples in this chapter. I want you to do that because I know you know them, and I want you to *see* results!

English Vocabulary and SAT Words

• • •

It's a Snap!

*I*f you've worked along with me, you've learned foreign-language vocabulary better than you ever have before. And you know how important that can be for you so far as the College Board achievement tests are concerned. Again, even if the systems didn't work, they would still work! That's because the bit of effort involved in trying to apply them *pinpoints* your concentration, *focuses* your attention, *forces* you to be Originally Aware. (It also *exercises* your imagination and observation.) Of course, the systems do work — exceptionally well, giving you one heck of a learning tool.

That tool is even easier to apply to English vocabulary. I've discussed how important it is to know English vocabulary for the SAT exams, whether you're answering antonym, synonym, or similar relationship questions. You know that Adam Robinson, coauthor of *Cracking the System*, says that knowing (memorizing) vocabulary is of utmost importance. Others do, too. A *New York Times* article by Edward B. Fiske mentions the "tricks" taught by *The Princeton Review* "that give clients an edge over other test takers." Those "tricks" are fine for those who *don't know the material*, although the Educational Testing Service suggests that encouraging students to rely on "what they see as tricks" rather than on substantive educational knowledge is, in effect, "the academic equivalent of providing steroids to athletes."

Well, let me show you a way to *know* the information — in this case, the vocabulary. John Katzman of *The Princeton Review* is among those quoted in the above-mentioned article. He acknowledges that, because the ETS is changing some of its testing techniques, he now spends "less time on test-taking techniques and more on teaching basic math and English." In my opinion, that means he realizes that students had better know (that is, remember) those basics. The test-preparation series *Cracking the System* "steals" a page from my book(s) when it mentions how helpful it is to memorize words via "the Image approach," using a "wild image."

The *Times* article, however, states that a *Princeton Review* trademark is its "hit parade" of words "that appeared frequently on past tests." And although the College Board (sponsors of the SAT) "insists that the testing service now makes a point of not repeating those words, . . . Katzman asserts — somewhat to his surprise — that the list still works."

That's why the words I'll use as examples are taken (with permission) directly from that "hit parade" list of frequently tested words. (Do you remember the meaning of *sycophant*, one of the hit-parade words I used as an example two chapters back? Perhaps you were *sick of* the *ant* that continually *flattered* you, that was being overly *servile*.)

A bit of imagination did it for you. The word *abeyance* means "temporary suspension." Your Substitute Word or thought for "abeyance" might be ants baying at the moon or a bay full of ants (*bay ants*). See a silly mental picture of ants baying while they are temporarily suspended in air and you'll have locked that word and its meaning into your memory. *Paleontology* is "the study of fossils." A large letter *E* is pale (*pale E*) and it is standing on top of a tall *G* (*pale E on tall G*). It's standing on the tall *G* so that it can study fossils. See that picture.

That's all there is to it. Now, work along with me on these hit-parade words:

> **Mitigate** — "to lessen the severity (of something)": *Mitt a gate* or *meet a gate*. You *meet a gate* that's in severe pain. You work on it and *lessen the severity* of the pain. (I won't keep repeating that you *must see* that picture; you know that now. I'll test you on the words later.)

Diligent — "hardworking": See a *dill* pickle being *a gent* and it's working very hard. Or, you're *working hard* at trying to *deal* cards to *a gent*.

Complacent — "smug; self-satisfied": You're asking a cent to come play with you (*come play, cent*), but it's acting very *smug*.

Blasphemy — "irreverent talk about God or religion": Can you visualize yourself proclaiming, "It's a *blast for me* to *speak irreverently about religion*"? Then do so. Or, you speak irreverently, and so on, and there's an explosion. You ask, "Is that *blast for me?*" (*Last for me* or *last form E* would also do.)

Meander — "to wander slowly": *Me and her* (see yourself with a female) are *wandering slowly*. This is logical, so make it ridiculous — for example, by seeing that both of you are wandering slowly among the treetops without touching the ground!

Emulate — "to imitate (usually something admired)": A gigantic letter *M* is late; you say, "*M, you late,*" as you *imitate* it because you admire it. Use a bit of imagination; actually see/hear yourself saying the words and doing the actions.

Supercilious — "haughty; arrogant": A donkey is acting super silly (*super silly ass*). It's also being extremely *haughty* and *arrogant*.

Bastion — "a stronghold or fortress": See a gigantic cup of tea on top of a *fortress* — that's the *best tea on* (the fortress).

Peripheral — "on the edge; surrounding": Either *pear rip for Al* (or *all*), or *pear* (or *pair*) *referral* would do fine as Substitute Words or phrases. Can you *connect* one of those to the meaning of the word? (Perhaps you take a gigantic pear, which you rip for [someone you know named] Al, but you rip it only around its edge; or you rip only the things *surrounding* the pear.)

Extol — "to praise": Associate *eggs toll*, *eggs told*, or *egg stole* to the definition of *extol*. There's a tollbooth where only eggs must stop and pay — it's an *eggs' toll*. It's doing so well that everyone rushes over to *praise* it.

Do you know these ten? I'll now list them in a different order; as you read or think about each one, its meaning will come to mind. If it doesn't, go back and strengthen your associations — then you'll surely know them all. Here they are:

emulate	*supercilious*
bastion	*complacent*
meander	*peripheral*
extol	*diligent*
blasphemy	*mitigate*

If you heard or read the definition, that would bring the word to mind. It always works both ways. Don't continue until you know these ten hit-parade words. Then, try another ten:

Acquiesce — "to give in; to agree": You *agree* to a key. A gigantic key is offered to you — "*A key? Yes.*" (Sounds enough like "acquiesce" to remind you of it.) See yourself *giving in* to the key, *agree*ing over and over again.

Desecrate — "to profane a holy place; to treat a sacred thing irreverently". You're in a desert and see a gigantic crate — *desert crate*. It's a sacred thing (perhaps a halo is over it), but you kick it and so forth — treat it with disrespect, irreverently. (*Dat's a crate* would also do.)

Atrophy — "to waste away from lack of use": *A trophy* or *I throw fee* will remind you of the pronunciation. Connect one of them to the meaning of the word. Perhaps visualize *a trophy* (a gigantic loving cup or statue) *wasting away* (shrinking) because no one ever uses it (see it covered with dust and spiderwebs).

Relegate — "to send to a lower position": You *roll a gate* downward, *sending it to a lower position*. Be sure you actually *see* that.

Candid — "honest; frank": A *can did* it and immediately confessed because it's so *honest* and *frank*. (*Candied* or *canned it* would also remind you of "candid"; or you could see someone taking secret *candid* snapshots and then admitting it *honestly*.)

Austere — "severely simple and plain; without frills": You're shouting at someone who's driving a *severely simple and plain* car, "*Aw, steer!*" (*Horse dear, horse steer, awes deer* are also good substitute phrases. Associate one of them to the meaning of the word. (A *horse* that's *dear* to you refuses all frills, it prefers to be *without frills*.)

Apocryphal — "untrue; invented": Visualize a pack (of cards) being riffle-shuffled (*a pack riffle*) in a way you just *invented*; but it's *untrue*, it's not really a riffle shuffle. *Apple cry* *fall* would also act as a reminder. You are listening to an *apple* continually *cry* that it's *fall*ing, but it's "crying wolf," it's *untrue*.

Repress — "to hold down; to hold back": You're pressing a wrinkled shirt over and over again — *re-pressing* it — and then to keep it from getting off the ironing board, you *hold it down*.

Incongruous — "out of place; not fitting in": See someone or something *in Congress* that stands out like a sore thumb — it's completely *out of place*.

Euphony — "pleasant sound (usually words)": Imagine someone saying very *pleasant-sounding words* (which echo all over the world, to make the picture ridiculous), but he's a phony (or funny), and you shout, *"You phony!"* (or *"You funny!"*).

If you've associated your Substitute Word or phrase for each to the meaning of each, the words should bring that meaning to mind. Try it:

repress	*acquiesce*
candid	*euphony*
desecrate	*atrophy*
austere	*apocryphal*
relegate	*incongruous*

And if you know these ten, go back to the first group of ten and look at each word as you cover the definition. You'll know those, too — as well as *sycophant, abeyance, plagiarize,* and *paleontology*. You can turn back and try the same thing with the foreign-vocabulary examples I used. Go ahead; impress yourself!

Obviously, I can't use *every* word as an example. And it's important that you apply the technique entirely on your own. Just grab a dictionary or any word list and *do* it. But before you do, I want you to be aware of the fact that you can apply the technique to prefixes (beginnings of words), stems (bodies of words), and suffixes (endings of words). Knowing the meanings of these parts will serve as a memory aid toward knowing the whole word. Just a few examples:

The prefix *sub* means "under." Picturing a *sub*marine going *under* water is, obviously, all you'd need. Just make it ridiculous in some way when you include it in an association. The prefix *per* means "through." See a gigantic *pear* walking *through* you. The prefix *poly* means "many." Just picture *many pollies* (parrots). The prefix *ex* means "out." See yourself *x*-ing something *out*.

You needn't specifically know the meaning of the prefix. Having a *picture* ready for it will help to form substitute thoughts for words. For example, I always visualize a convict (a man in the traditional striped prison garb) when I see the prefix *con*. So, for the words *conciliate*, *condescend*, and *concise*, you might visualize a *con* being *silly* while he *ate*, a *con descend*ing, and a *con's eyes*, respectively. Each would be associated to its meaning, of course.

The stem *chron* means "time." Picture a king wearing a clock (*time*) instead of a *crown*. The stem *clam* means "to shout." See and hear a *clam shouting*. *Culp* means "blame." Someone is *blaming* you for something and it makes you *gulp*. *Belli* means "war." Picture a *war* being fought on your *belly*. *Rupt* is "to break." See yourself having *rubbed* something in order *to break* it.

The suffix *ward* means "in the direction of." Picture an entire hospital *ward* moving in your *direction*. The suffix *ose* or *ous* means "full of" or "given to." See a *house* crammed *full of* anything being *given to* you. *Atrist* means "one who practices." Imagine yourself *practicing a twist*, or *at* your *wrist*.

Think about it for a moment — to learn that *prodigal* means "wasteful," just "see" yourself about to *prod a gal* and when you do, she *wastes* away; or see a *pro dig all* the dirt, and the dirt he digs goes to *waste*. To know that *stagnant* means "not moving": you're tagging an ant (*tag ant*) and it's easy, because the ant's *not moving*, it's standing still.

This method is a thousand times easier — and certainly much more fun and creative — than trying to learn these words with rote memory.

Questions and Answers

Q. Why does the Substitute Word System make it easier to learn English- and foreign-language vocabulary?

A. If you've worked along with me up to here, if you've read just the last two paragraphs before this question-and-answer section, you certainly know the answer. Aside from forcing attention and Original Awareness, as I've told you a few times, the system forces you to apply the basic memory rule: **Associate something new to something you already know.**

Q. What if I can't think of a word or phrase that sounds exactly like the word I want to learn?

A. Get as close as you can to the sound of the new word. Some foreign words may contain sounds that we don't have in English. It doesn't matter; get as close as possible. It doesn't have to be exact. If *you* think of it, it will remind you of the word. I used *écureuil* as an example. We don't have the exact French *"euil"* sound in English. Yet the Substitute Word System enabled you to remember it. "Role a gate" is not the exact sound of *relegate,* nor is "in Congress" the exact sound of *incongruous,* but they sure will remind you of the words.

True memory tells you the exact sound of the word. My systems are really only aids to your true memory. True memory is the associative process with which you're born. It's the process that makes you think "up" when you hear "down," and "black" when you hear "white," "hot" when you hear "cold," and so forth. There's a very thin line between the true memory and a trained memory. As you continue to use the systems, that line starts to fade; it gets thinner and thinner. Your mind already is an *associating machine.* I'm not giving you anything new, I'm just improving to an incredible degree what you already have!

Q. Will the Substitute Word System help me remember any words in any language?

A. There is no limit to how many or what kind of words you can remember (learn) by applying the technique. Before you knew the technique, you tried to remember new words using rote memory. You might as well make it easy for yourself and use the system.

Q. What about tough languages like Chinese or Japanese?

A. What difference does it make? It may be true that it will always be more difficult to learn those languages — whether or not you apply my system. But try a few examples. *Konichiwa* means "hello" in Japanese. See an ice-cream cone scratching because it's itchy; you approach and ask where it itches (*cone itchy where*) as you say hello. *Nee how mah?* is "How are you?" in Mandarin. Associate *knee how ma* to that. There's no doubt that applying the system to foreign-language vocabulary makes that vocabulary easier to learn, no matter which language it is.

Q. Can I apply the same idea to foreign phrases?

A. I've already touched on that. Sure you can! *Comment allez-vous?* means "How are you?" in French. You're shaking hands with someone ("How are you?"), as you say, *"Come on,"* and take him into an *alley* to show him the *view* (*Come on, alley view — Comment allez-vous?*). *Rien de grave* is a French idiomatic expression meaning "(It's) not serious." Associate *ran the grave* and *not serious*.

Q. What about the pronunciation of foreign words?

A. That's really not a problem. The assumption must be that if you're studying a foreign language, you already know the basics — the alphabet and correct pronunciations. And again, true memory comes into play: knowing or remembering the word *means* knowing the pronunciation, too. You select your Substitute Word in the first place because it reminds you of the pronunciation of the word you want to learn.

Q. Can a Substitute Word be found for *any* word, in any language?

A. You can always come up with something, even a thought that you can't put into words, that will be close enough to any word to remind you of it. And just thinking about a new English word or a new foreign one (in order to come up with a Substitute Word, phrase, or thought) impresses that new word into your memory!

Chapter 11

Names and Numbers and Dates

• • •

And Presidents of the United States

*Y*ou'll be amazed at what you can memorize by applying what you've already learned. You can manipulate and twist the ideas in order to solve almost any memory/learning problem. (You'll learn one more major concept two chapters down the pike.) And you can learn whatever information you like, the way *you* want to or feel you have to. I'll use the presidents of the United States as an example. I received different answers from students attending different schools — even different classes at the same school — when I asked about the presidents. "No, we don't need to remember the presidents at all." "Yes, we have to remember all the presidents." "We have to know them in sequence." "We only have to know which years they were in office." (That's pretty close to knowing them in sequence.) "We have to know them by number." And more.

I asked *Cracking the System* coauthor Adam Robinson: "Do you think I should simply teach how to remember the presidents in all ways, and then let the student make his or her own decision?"

"Of course," he answered. "Just as someone studying art should be exposed to all possible techniques so that the student/artist can decide which he wants to use. Teach how to remember the presidents in order and by number, and the dates, and so on. Let him decide which to apply." I agree. And even if you don't have to remember the presidents at all, learn the idea, because you'll be able to apply it to information you *do* have to remember. In addition, you'll be learning a new concept or two.

The first thing to know is how to "handle" the *names* of the presidents. Well, you already know how: use the Substitute Word technique. A name is usually a conglomeration of sound, as is any unfamiliar word. A Substitute Word for Washington would be either *wash* or *washing*. (*Washing* a *ton* of clothes is fine, but not really necessary. *Washing* alone would suffice.)

To know the presidents sequentially is easy and fun. Just make up a Substitute Word for each and Link them. You can do that; and *after* you've learned them, go back and associate each Substitute Word to another word that will *tell* you that president's years of service. I'll explain that in a moment, after you've seen the "presidential list." You can also memorize all the presidents by number. In order to do that, you need to know the Peg Words up to number 41. (If you don't, go back and learn them now because I know you'll want to try this.) I'll help you with the first eight presidents — all the different ways to "learn" them. Then I'll suggest Substitute Words and associations, and you're on your own.

George Washington was the first U.S. president. You know how to visualize "Washington," but how will you know that he was number 1? You know how to do that, too. You have a Peg Word now that represents number 1, that *means* number 1. All you have to do is associate your Substitute Word for the name to your Peg Word for number 1 — *tie*. See yourself *washing* your gigantic *tie* while you're still wearing it; or, you're wearing a *washing* machine instead of a *tie*. *See* the picture you select.

Second president: John Adams. *Adam, atom, Adam's* apple, are all good Substitute Words. If you thought of Adam (as in Adam and Eve), a *fig leaf*, which is what Adam allegedly wore, would also act as a reminder. Perhaps you see a man with a long, gray beard (*Noah* — number 2) and millions of people are rushing *at 'im*. Come up with your own silly picture, and *see* it.

Third president: Thomas Jefferson. You can see a *nickel* (because, Jefferson is pictured on that coin). You can imagine yourself asking your *ma* (number 3), *"D'ja have a son?"* *Shiver son* or *chef's son* are good. If you use *nickel*, see your *ma's* picture on it. There are so many ways to go. Select one and see it.

Fourth president: James Madison. *Medicine* is a good Substitute Word. You can visualize a loaf of *rye* (number 4) bread (or a bottle of rye whiskey) being given *medicine*. You can see *Madison* Avenue paved with *rye* bread. *Mad at son* would also do. *See* the picture you select.

Fifth president: James Monroe. Your Peg Word is *law*. You could use *man row* or Marilyn *Monroe* or *Monroe* Doctrine to remind you of the president's name. See Marilyn Monroe dressed as (and acting like) a policeman or a judge, according to what you're using to represent *law*.

Sixth president: John Quincy Adams. Use the Substitute Word you used for the second president. This time, associate it to your Peg Word for number 6 — *shoe*. Perhaps Adam is wearing a *shoe* instead of a *fig leaf* in the Garden of Eden.

Seventh president: Andrew Jackson. Your Peg Word is *cow*. Associate that to *jack* (a car jack, or jacks that children play with) or to entertainer Michael *Jackson*. It's up to you. Perhaps you're using a *jack* (and a smaller one — its *son* — if you think you need it) to lift a *cow*. Or, you're milking a cow and millions of *jacks* come out instead of milk. See your picture.

Eighth president: Martin Van Buren. A picture in your mind of only a *van* would do it, because no other president has a "van" in his last name, but you can use *bureau*, or use both. Perhaps you open your *bureau* and a *van* filled with *ivy* (8) comes out and runs over you.

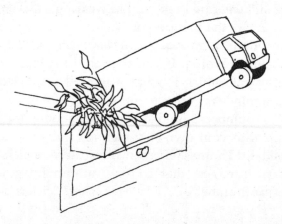

You might prefer to see millions of *vans* growing on a college wall instead of *ivy*. Select one of these or one you thought of yourself — and *see it*.

If you've really made the associations, you *know* the information. Prove it to yourself; fill in these blanks:

Jackson was # _____   Monroe was # _____

Madison was # _____   Jefferson was # _____

Washington was # _____ Adams was president # _____

Van Buren was # _____   and # _____

And see how rapidly you can answer these:

president #4 = _____ president #7 = _____

president #1 = _____ president #3 = _____

president #8 = _____ president #5 = _____

president #6 = _____ president #2 = _____

You can know *all* the presidents in a short time, easily. You can enjoy learning them and can retain the information for as long as you like. Here's the list from number 9 to number 41. I'll suggest a Substitute Word for each and mention the Peg Word (although you should know them). Make up your own silly pictures. In parentheses, I'll tell you the year that each took office. **Don't** try to memorize those dates. For now, learn only last name and numerical position (even if you don't need this information, do it anyway, just as a good exercise). I'll talk about first (given) names, the dates, and other "presidential" information afterward. I'd suggest that you do a few presidents, stop to review (just see each silly picture again), then do some more, and so on.

9. William Harrison (1841) .... *bee* to *hairy* (or *hurry*) *son*

10. John Tyler (1841) .... *toes* to *tiler* (one who tiles)

11. James Polk (1845) .... *tot* to *poke*

12. Zachary Taylor (1849) .... *tin* to *tailor*

13. Millard Fillmore (1850) .... *tomb* to *fill more; feel more*

14. Franklin Pierce (1853) .... *tire* to *pierce*

15. James Buchanan (1857) .... *towel* to *blue* (or *blew*) *cannon*

16. Abraham Lincoln (1861) .... *dish* to *penny* or *link on*

17. Andrew Johnson (1865) .... *tack* to *yawn* (and *son*); *jaw son*

18. Ulysses S. Grant (1869) .... *dove* to *granite, grand, grant*

19. Rutherford B. Hayes (1877) .... *tub* to *hay* or *haze*

20. James A. Garfield (1881) .... *nose* to *cigar field* or *car field*

21. Chester A. Arthur (1881) .... *net* to *author* or *ah there*

22. Grover Cleveland (1885) .... *nun* to *cleave* (or *leave*) *land*

23. Benjamin Harrison (1889) .... *name* to *hairy* (or *hurry*) *son*

24. Grover Cleveland (1893) .... *Nero* to *cleave* (or *leave*) *land*

25. William McKinley (1897) .... *nail* to *Mack in lea, me can lie*

26. Theodore Roosevelt (1901) .... *notch* to *rose* or *rose felt*

27. William Howard Taft (1909) .... *neck* to *daft, taffy,* or *raft*

28. Woodrow Wilson (1913) .... *knife* to *will son* or *wills on*

29. Warren G. Harding (1921) .... *knob* to *hard ink* or *hardening*

30. Calvin Coolidge (1923) .... *mouse* to *cool ledge* or *cool itch*

31. Herbert Hoover (1929) .... *mat* to *Hoover* vacuum, *who where,* or *hoof air*

32. Franklin D. Roosevelt (1933) .... *moon* to *rose* or *rose felt*

33. Harry S. Truman (1945) .... *mummy* to *true* (*threw*) *man*

34. Dwight D. Eisenhower (1953) ...... *mower* to *I send hour* (*clock*) or *ice in hour*

35. John F. Kennedy (1961) .... *mule* to *can of D's; can a day*

36. Lyndon B. Johnson (1963) .... *match* to *john* and *son; jaw and son*

37. Richard M. Nixon (1969) .... *mug* to *nicks on* or *nick sun*

38. Gerald Ford (1974) .... *movie* to *a Ford* (car)

39. Jimmy Carter (1977) .... *mop* to *car tear* or *cart air*

40. Ronald Reagan (1981) .... *rose* to *ray again* (or just *ray*)

41. George Bush (1989) .... *rod* to *bush*

Have you really tried to form an association for each? Fine; now number a sheet of paper from 1 to 41 and list all the presidents! If you don't want to bother with paper and pencil, do it mentally. Count from 1 to 41 *using your Peg Words*. As you think of each Peg Word, the president's name for that numerical position will come to mind. Stop reading for a while now, and *try* it.

If you know the presidents from 1 to 41, you also know them *out of order*, by number (as you do the first eight). Test yourself; you'll see that this is so. There's nothing to it once you understand the Substitute Word idea and once you know the Phonetic Number/ Alphabet and the Peg Words. Now, I suggested that you use a Substitute Word for the last name only. The assumption is that you *know* the entire name and that all you need is the reminder. As a matter of fact, you probably need only *part* of the last name as the reminder. *Ice* or *eyes* would be enough to remind you of Eisenhower. *You* have to make those decisions.

If you want to be reminded of the first name — no problem. Make up a Substitute Word for the first name and get *that* into the picture. If you originally used the picture of a *mummy throw*ing a *man* to remember that Truman was the 33d president, you can see either the *mummy* or the *man* (or both) being very *hairy*. That's enough to remind you of Harry. (You'll learn how to handle letters of the alphabet — for the middle initial *S* — shortly.)

The 11th president was *James* Polk. You may have visualized yourself *pok*ing a *tot* (I'd see the finger going *through* the tot to make the picture silly). If you also visualized yourself *aim*ing that finger, that would remind you of James (*aims*). To differentiate between John Adams and John Quincy Adams, get *win see, win C, quit see,* or *wins E* into your association for the 6th president.

Eventually, you'll have "standards" for first names. (I *always* use *aims* for James.) For William — a yam writing its will, *will yam; robber* for Robert; *sack carry* for Zachary; and so forth. You can get anything you like into your association — a Substitute Word for a president's wife, child, or vice president. The picture of a *mouse* (30) on a *cool ledge* tells you that Coolidge was the 30th president. Get *doors* into that picture to remind you that (Charles G.) Dawes was his vice president. See those doors *charred* or having *quarrels* to remind you of *Charles.*

If you need to know the dates or years of service, use a word that tells you the date phonetically, but *not* the Peg Word. The reason is that if you've used the Peg Words to tell you the numerical positions, using some again for dates *may* be confusing. (If you only Linked the presidents, then of course you can use the Peg Words for the dates.) So, in your association for Polk include **rail** or **reel** to tell you that Polk took office in **1845**. (You *know* it wasn't **1945**.)

Get **ripe** or **reap** (because **R** = 4 and **P** = 9) into your Zachary Taylor association to tell you he took office in **1849**. In the Fillmore picture, include **lass, loose,** or **lice** (**1850**). And **loom** or **lime** in the Franklin Pierce association tells you **1853**.

If the dates are important to you, and if you learn them for all the presidents, you'll also automatically know the *number of years* each president was in office. Simple arithmetic does it. Since Polk took office in 1845 and Taylor took office in 1849, then Polk served a single four-year term. Fillmore took office in 1850, so Taylor served only *one* year. Pierce took office in 1853; so Fillmore served as president for *three* years. Look over the dates in the list and it all becomes crystal clear in minutes.

I'll be talking about more fascinating date memory in the next chapter and in chapter 14.

Chapter 12

American History

· · ·

*No Problem Learning Events
and Their Dates*

$\mathcal{S}$ome students tell me that it is no longer necessary to remember specific dates (it sure was when I went to school); some say that it's definitely necessary, and others tell me that even if it isn't necessary, it's a plus to do so. What many teachers insist on is that the student remember the sequence of events, not the dates themselves. Well, I can't think of a better way to establish a sequence of events than to know the dates. That's what dates *do*: they establish a sequence of events!

I've just discussed names and numbers. Names have to be remembered not only where people are concerned. Things and places have names, too.

It may not be particularly useful to you to remember the precise years in which specific states were admitted to the Union. It could be useful if certain significant world events occurred at about the same time. Fine. Associate the significant event with the state and the date. That's up to you. Right now, see how easy it is to memorize a state and its date of admission. Just make up a Substitute Word for the state and associate it to a word or phrase that represents the date. There's usually no need to bother with the century digits, because most of the dates are in the late 1700s or in the 1800s. You need a word to remind you of the *year*. You can use your Peg Word, or any word that fits phonetically. Form your own pictures for the following:

Vermont was admitted to the Union in 1791. Visualize *vermin*

(Vermont) filling a gigantic **pot**. For the entire year, took pot will do (T=1, K=7, P=9, T=1).

Kentucky — 1792. You *can't talk* because there's a **duck** bone in your throat — or just *bone* (your Peg Word) for '92.

Tennessee — 1796. Associate *ten, I see* or *tennis see* with **badge** or **dog bush**.

Indiana — 1816; *Indian* to *dish*.

Illinois — 1818; a picture of a *dove* that's *ill* will do it.

Maine — 1820. Associate water *main* with *nose;* or **divans** for the full year. You could even use **vans**, since you know that the first digit is a 1.

Minnesota — 1858; Link *mini soda* with *lava* or **leaf** or **love**.

Associating *color a toe* (or just *color* or *collar*) with *cage* or **cash** will tell you that Colorado was admitted to the Union in 1876.

You can put any information you want to into each association. You won't realize how well it works, however, if you only *read*. You have to *do* what I suggest in order to see that.

It isn't usually necessary for you to know the day and month of a historical event — but you can if you want to. I've devised a simple system wherein one word (or a phrase) will *tell* you those two pieces of information. The word or phrase must begin with the consonant sound that represents the vital month's numerical position (May is the 5th month, for example). The next consonant sound(s) can tell you the day of the month (1 to 31), and the following consonant sound(s) would tell you the year. So you can form a word or phrase to tell you anything *you* want it to tell you.

Assume you want to remember that Neil Armstrong was the first man to step onto the moon, and that the event took place in 1969. Picture a very *strong arm* (Armstrong) stepping from a **ship** ('69) onto the moon.

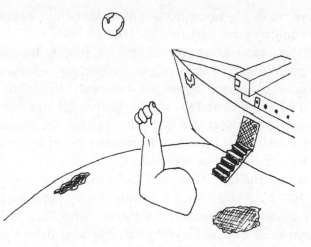

If you need day and month, you can see the arm stepping onto millions of **cans** (720 — 7th month, 20th day). For only month and year, **ketchup** is perfect (769 — 7th month of 1969).

There are other ways. You could make up a word or thought to represent each month of the year and get that into your picture whenever needed. For example, a *may*pole could always represent *May*; firecrackers or a *jewel* could always represent *July*. *Gust* of wind — Au*gust*; *junitor* — *January*; *ape* or showers — *April*; and so on. You'll have to decide which idea to use where. I want you to be aware of the possibilities so that you can make those decisions. Obviously, use what *works best for you*.

I'll suggest Substitute Words and pictures for the historical events listed below. Remember that you're always better off doing it on your own. Use your pictures or mine, but *do* it. Again, it's important, to me and to you, that you understand what you can accomplish. I'll test you afterward, so *see* the pictures.

- Custer's "last stand" occurred on June 25, 1876.

  See a lot of *custard* (or *cussed her*) crossing the **channel** (625 — 6th month, 25th day — June 25), carrying lots of **cash** ('76).
- The first message over the first telegraph line was sent on May 24, 1844.

  Imagine a telegraph wire rowing (*rower* — '44) to the

moon, making a **lunar** (524 — May 24) trip. You know that this couldn't have occurred in 1744 or 1944.

• The Magna Carta was signed by King John in the year 1215.

A gigantic *magnet* attracts a *car* (*magnet car* — Magna Carta) and a *king*, wearing a *john* for a crown (King John) signs it as he's having **dental** (1215) work done. If you think it important to know that King John signed the document at Runnymede, just include a Substitute Word to remind you of that — perhaps, *runny meat*.

• Alexander the Great invaded India in 327 BC.

If you think you need a reminder for BC, get a **Bic** pen into your association. Visualize someone who likes to *lick sand* (Alexander); he thinks it's *great*. He also drinks *india* ink while wearing **mink** (327). **Manic, monk,** or **my neck** would also do.

• William Shakespeare was born on April 26, 1564.

You're on a **ranch** (426 — April 26), *shaking* a *spear* in a **tall jar** (1564).

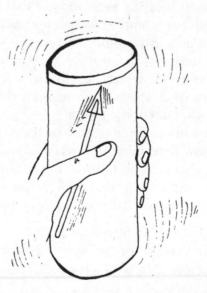

If only month and year are important to you, **rattle jar** or **rattle chair** (4-1564) would do it.

• Alaska was purchased from Russia on March 30, 1867.

You're purchasing a baked *Alaska* (or *I'll ask her*, or *last car*), which is filled with **mums** (330 — March 30), and you're paying with a gigantic **check** ('67).
- Julius Caesar was assassinated in 44 BC.

  Visualize a *Caesar* salad being stabbed (with a **Bic** pen, if you think it necessary) and letting out a **roar** ('44). *Sees air* or *cease air* would also do.
- Joan of Arc led the French armies against England in 1429.

  A gigantic **turnip** (1429) *owns* an *ark* (Joan of Arc — or *john dark* for Jean D'Arc) and leads it to *land* (England).
- Benjamin Franklin flew his famous kite on June 15, 1752.

  A gigantic *frank*furter (Franklin) is on a **shuttle** (or use **show tell**; 615 — June 15), flying a kite that he's **ticklin'** (1752). If you know the century, your Peg Word, *lion*, would be all you'd need.
- Lincoln delivered his Gettysburg Address on November 19, 1863.

  You might see a gigantic Lincoln penny *getting his burg*er (Gettysburg), which is all **tied** with **tape** (1119 — November 19) and which he spreads with *jam* ('63).

Review your associations; simply go back and see each picture clearly. Then fill in the dates for these events:

Alexander the Great invaded India in _____.

The first message over the first telegraph line was sent on _____.

Alaska was purchased from Russia on _____.

Custer's last stand occurred on _____.

Julius Caesar was assassinated in _____.

Lincoln delivered his Gettysburg address on _____.

The Magna Carta was signed in the year _____ by _____ at _____.

Joan of Arc led the French armies into England in _____.

William Shakespeare was born on _____.

Benjamin Franklin flew his kite on _____.

Convinced? Good. Here are some more historical facts to

practice with and to show you how great your memory is. Memorize them even if you don't have to know them for school. It's good practice for you.

- In 1519, Magellan of Spain sailed around the world.

    Tilt up or **tall top** transposes to 1519. A tall top is *mad* and *yellin'* (Magellan) because it's in *pain* (Spain). The pain is caused by sailing *around the world*. I've included all the facts; you include only those things you want to be reminded of.
- In 1961, Gagarin of Russia went around the earth in space.

    A gigantic *sheet* ('61) is being used as a *gag*, but some *air* gets *in* (*gag air in* — Gagarin). The person with the gag *rushes* (Russia) into *space* and goes *around the earth*.

The next three events happened in the 1800s; if you know that, then all you need in your association is a word to represent the last two digits.

- Washington, D.C., became the capital of the United States in 1800.

    Your **sis** ('00) is *washing* the dome of a capitol building.
- In 1807, Robert Fulton sailed his steamboat, the *Clermont*.

    A steamboat comes out of a **sack** ('07) and — if you want to remember the name of Fulton's boat — goes *clear* up a *mount*ain.
- The battle of the Alamo happened in 1836.

    Just see a gigantic *match* (Peg Word for 36) fighting other matches — they're *all* named *Moe* (Alamo); or picture *a lamb, oh*.

You can use your Peg Words in your associations or other words that fit phonetically. It doesn't matter. The thing to do, usually, is to use the first thing that comes to mind. Most of the time, that's best.

Occasionally, you'll come across an almost logical (and obvious) association to help you learn a specific piece of information. For example, President **Van** Buren was born in 1782. *Van* tells you his name as well as the last two digits of his birth year.

Abraham Lincoln was born in 1809. **Abe** transposes to 9; that helps you remember the year. Benjamin Franklin's birth year is 1706; he was considered to be a **sage**. Lincoln was assassinated in 1865; see the perpetrators — millions of them — being forced into *jail*. Napoleon was crowned emperor in 1804; see the crown being so heavy that it makes his head **sore**. See the *Titanic* sinking because it's made of *tin* to remind you of 1912. (If you feel you need the century digits, see it sinking in a *tub*.)

This one has nothing to do with dates, but the last three letters of Abra*ham Lin*coln's first name and the first three letters of his last name tell you the name of his first-term vice president — *Hamlin*.

Don't take the time to look for this sort of thing. If you happen to spot one, fine; but be sure to make it ridiculous; not all of the above are. I've touched on them only because they're interesting. Generally, you're better off applying the systems as we've been doing. Bear in mind that the more you apply (use) them, the easier it will be to apply them!

In the next short chapter, I'll teach you that one remaining concept I mentioned earlier. Then we'll "do" some more history — some more facts, events, dates.

Chapter 13

So You Think You Know Your ABCs

• • •

*L*etters of the alphabet are as difficult to remember as numbers because they're really nothing but designs and they don't readily create pictures in your mind. That's why most people don't really know their ABCs. Can you recite the alphabet backward? Can you instantly name the 12th letter of the alphabet? The 21st? The 16th?

Well, it *is* possible to visualize the letters, and to know their positions, if you want to. The idea for picturing them is so simple and so obvious you can learn it in minutes. Since it will be important for you to remember letters — for equations, formulas, spelling, and more — I suggest you spend the necessary few minutes.

All you need to do is decide on a word that sounds like each letter (just as in the Substitute Word System) and picture that word to represent the letter from now on! For **A**, I always see an *ape*; for **B**, I picture a *bean* (I don't use *bee* because that's a basic Peg Word — for 9); for **C**, see the *sea*; for **D**, a college *dean* or a *deal* (playing cards); and so forth. Here's my full list (in a moment I'll explain why there's a Peg Word before each letter):

(tie)	A — ape
(Noah)	B — bean
(ma)	C — sea
(rye)	D — dean, deal
(law)	E — eel
(shoe)	F — half, *effort, effervescent*
(cow)	G — jeans, jeep
(ivy)	H — age, itch, ache

(bee)	I — eye
(toes)	J — jail, jaybird
(tot)	K — cake, cane
(tin)	L — el (elevated train)
(tomb)	M — hem, *emperor*
(tire)	N — hen
(towel)	O — old, eau (water), owe, open
(dish)	P — pea
(tack)	Q — cue (stick)
(dove)	R — art, hour (clock)
(tub)	S — ess curve
(nose)	T — tea, tee (golf)
(net)	U — ewe, youth
(nun)	V — veal, V (victory sign)
(name)	W — Waterloo
(Nero)	X — eggs, exit, X-ray
(nail)	Y — wine, whine, wife
(notch)	Z — zebra

Change a word here and there if you want to; just be sure that the word can be pictured and that it sounds like the letter. If you're using *hour* for **R**, visualize a clock; for Waterloo, picture Napoleon. You can, if you'd rather, use *trouble you* for **W** and picture yourself in trouble. Go over the list a few times and you'll "have" them. And then, whenever you have to remember a letter, simply put the word that represents that letter into your association.

You can also use these "letter words" as alternate Peg Words from 1 to 26. That's why I placed the basic Peg Word for the letter's position in front of each. As long as you now know 26 letter words, why *not* use them as an alternate Peg list (just in case you want to remember two sets of information by number at the same time)? The problem is that you have to know the numerical position of the letter in order for the letter word to serve that purpose. So, associate *tie* to *ape* and you'll know that **A** is the first letter because *ape* represents **A** and *tie* represents 1.

Associate *towel* to *old* and you'll always know that **O** is the 15th letter. See a *tub* going around an *ess* curve and you'll know that **S** is the 19th letter of the alphabet. Do that with each letter, down to a large *notch* in a *zebra*, and you'll know the numerical position of every letter. (Think of your basic Peg Words from 26 to 1 and you'll be able to say the alphabet backward.)

Now each letter represents a number in your mind, just as your basic Peg Words do. What you associate with *hem* would be number 13. Although you could memorize two lists of items at the same time using your basic Peg Words, using those for one list and the letter words for the other might avoid a bit of confusion at first. A much more important use for the letter words is when you're trying to learn something with more than one "4" (or whatever) in it, like a mathematical formula. Then you could use *rye* to remind you of one 4 and, to avoid confusion, *dean* to remind you of the other 4.

There are many ways to create Peg Word lists. The basic Peg list, based on the Phonetic Number/Alphabet, is by far the best — it's unlimited. The letter-word list is good for emergencies, even though it only goes up to 26. There's one I teach to children in minutes that enables them to remember up to ten items. But it's not only for children; learn this — it will come in quite handy. It's based on "The Children's Marching Song," a song most of us know.

"This old man, number one, he played knick-knack on a gun . . ." The words *rhyme* with the numbers. (I don't use "gun" when I teach this to small children — I use "run." You may want to change to that, too.) I've changed a few of the other words for different reasons — mainly because I didn't want them to conflict with other words you might already be using.

1. gun	6. sticks
2. glue	7. heaven
3. tree	8. gate
4. door	9. vine
5. hive	10. pen

The original word for 2 in the song is *shoe*; can't use that because it'd conflict with your basic Peg Word for number 6. The truth is that it doesn't really matter; you'll *know* which Peg list you're using and you'll automatically know which number a word represents.

There are ways to expand this up-to-ten list (*leaven* for 11, *shelf* for 12), but you're better off using it as is, when you need another word to represent a small number. I'll show you one way in the next chapter, where I'll discuss some more events, facts, and dates.

Chapter 14

World History

• • •

English Rulers, Chinese Dynasties, Wars, and More

Knowing the sequence of the United States presidents and the years during which they served is a great help when studying American history. Knowing the kings and queens of England the same way is helpful when you're studying world history. Again, I can't select examples that are pertinent specifically and only for you. The best I can do is to choose examples that are pertinent for most of the students to whom I've spoken. And — much more important — I can select examples that teach you a concept, a *technique* that can be applied to other information of a similar nature that *is* relevant to you specifically. So, learn the following nine reigns with me whether or not you need to know the information now. Look them over first — from 1760 to the present:

> George III: 1760–1820
> George IV: 1820–1830
> William IV: 1830–1837
> Victoria: 1837–1901
> Edward VII: 1901–1910
> George V: 1910–1936
> Edward VIII: 1936
> George VI: 1936–1952
> Elizabeth II: 1952–present

Now, you have to make a decision; if you feel that the sequence alone is all you'd need in order to get good grades, fine — Link the names. (*Gorge ma* — George III; *gorge rye* — George IV; *will yam rye* — William IV; and so on.) It's probably easier for you to know them by number; the Peg technique is slightly more definite. You can use your basic Peg Words from 1 to 9 (*tie* to *bee*), or the letter words (*ape* to *eye*), or the rhyming words (*gun* to *vine*). Let's use the rhyming words (just so that you can see how well they work).

And there's another choice, for the dates: you can use a word that reminds you of only the last two digits of the year, or a word that tells you the last three digits (since you know that all the dates start with a 1). **Catches**, for example, transposes to 760; you'd know that it means 1760.

Catches *nose* could represent the years of George III's reign. Catches is 1760 and nose is 20, which could mean only 1820. Another way, if you know you're starting in 1760, is to put a word into your association that tells you the total number of years the monarch ruled. George III reigned for 60 years. Get *cheese* into your picture. Simple arithmetic will tell you the exact dates.

Let's assume that you want to know the rulers by number, and also the dates of their reigns. Also assume that all you need to know are the last two digits of the years and that you'll use the rhyming ("Children's Marching Song") Peg Words. Let's do it quickly:

1 (gun). See a *gorge* with your *ma* in it (George III); your ma has a *gun*.

(Using *ma* won't confuse you into thinking that this is the third item, because you know you're using *gun, glue,* and so on for numerical position.) The gun shoots *cheese* ('60) into her *nose* ('20). This association will tell you that the first listing (*gun*) is George III (*gorge ma*) and that he reigned from 1760 to 1820 (*cheese nose*). See the picture clearly and you'll know the information.

2 (glue). George IV: 1820 to 1830. A gigantic loaf of *rye* bread is in a *gorge* (George IV). Associate that to *glue,* and that to, say, **no sums** ('20–'30).

3 (tree). William IV: 1830 to 1837. A *yam* is writing its *will* on a bottle of *rye* (William IV). Connect that to *tree,* and that to **messy mug** ('30–'37).

4 (door). Victoria: 1837 to 1901. A *door* makes the *victory* sign (Victoria). Associate that with **my guest** or **make suit** or **mixed** ('37–'01).

5 (hive). Edward VII: 1901 to 1910. A *hive* of bees is attacking a hospital *ward* that has a *cow* in it (Edward VII). Associate that with, perhaps, **acid heads** or **sad** *toes* ('01–'10). If you feel that *hive* will conflict with your basic Peg Word for 9 (*bee*), use only the hive in your picture, not the insect. If you'd rather, change the word to *jive* or *dive.*

6 (sticks). George V: 1910 to 1936. A bunch of *sticks* are in a *gorge* and a policeman (*law* — 5) arrests them (George V). Associate that with **toss my** *shoe* or **this much** or **ties** *match* ('10–'36).

7 (heaven). Edward VIII: 1936. Picture a hospital *ward* full of *ivy* (Edward VIII) in *heaven.* Associate that with **mash** or *match* ('36). Of course, if you wanted to, you could use *tub match* to give you all four digits in the year.

8 (gate). George VI: 1936 to 1952. A gigantic *shoe* is in a *gorge* (George VI); the shoe kicks a gigantic *gate.* Associate that with **my jawline** or *match lion* or **Michelin** or **Magellan** ('36–'52).

9 (vine). Elizabeth II: 1952 to the present. Someone *lays a bed* (Elizabeth) onto a *vine; Noah* (for "the Second") or a long, gray beard is sleeping in it. Associate that with **line,** *lion,* or **loan** ('52).

If you've really visualized the pictures, you know the material. Try it; test yourself. You'll see that it's so. I used *gorge* as the Substitute Word for George; that's okay, but, obviously, you can use whatever you like. *Jaws, gorge*ous, or *gorge* as in "gorge yourself with food" would also do. For Edward, you could have used *bed ward*. Remember that the thoughts that come to you first are usually the best ones for *you*.

You can apply the same basic techniques to the major Romanov rulers (imperial dynasty) of Russia, a topic taught in tenth- or eleventh-grade social studies. You have the same choices so far as handling the dates is concerned. Do what's best for you.

> Michael: 1613 to 1645
> Alexis: 1645 to 1676
> Peter I (the Great): 1689 to 1725
> Catherine II (the Great): 1762 to 1796
> Paul I: 1796 to 1801
> Alexander I: 1801 to 1825
> Nicholas I: 1825 to 1855
> Alexander II: 1855 to 1881
> Alexander III: 1881 to 1894
> Nicholas II: 1894 to 1917

Remembering 613–45 would tell you that the reign was from 1613 to 1645. For the first czar, then, you could picture a *mike* (microphone) in a *hall* (*mike hall* — Michael) and you **sh**oot h**im** (613) and make him *roll* (45). Michael of Russia ruled from 1613 to 1645.

Eggs or *legs* could be your Substitute Word for Alexis. Associate either one with, say, **shrill cash** (645–76).

A *great* letter *P tear*ing a *tie* tells you the name (Peter the First, or the Great). See that tie shaving a pie with a nail (**shave pie** *nail* — 689–25).

A *great cat run*ning (Catherine the Great) through *Noah*'s (the Second) beard tells you the name. The cat runs into the **kitchen** (or use **cushion** — 762) and hides behind a **bush** (96). If you don't need a reminder for "the Second" or for "the Great," all you'd need to "see" is a cat running into the kitchen that's behind a bush.

See yourself *pull* (Paul) your *tie* (the First) and a **cabbage** (796) falls out of it onto your **suit** (01).

A *sander* (Alexander) is sanding a ha**t** (the First). Yes, you could use *tie*, but when I have to use a word for the same number a few times, I occasionally use a different word that fits phonetically. The hat is being sanded very **fast** (801), for the **final** (825, or **funnel**) time.

A gigantic *nickel* (Nicholas) is wearing a ha**t** (the First) made of **vinyl** (825) with a large *lily* (55) on it.

A *sander* (Alexander) is sanding *Noah*'s beard (the Second) until it has a **full hole** (855) of *fat* (81) in it. (**Filial** or **flail** are fine for 855.)

Your *ma* (the Third) is a *fat* **pear** (or **avid bear** — 81–94) and you're *sanding* (Alexander) it.

Noah (the Second) is counting *nickels* (Nicholas) that go up in **vapor** (894) until you *tack* (17) them down (or use **paddock** for 917).

Apply the same technique to learning the dynasties of China. This time I'll let you handle the dates on your own, but I'll help you a bit with the Substitute Words. Look at this shortened list:

> Prehistoric China
> Chou Dynasty: 1027 to 256 BC
> Ch'in Dynasty: 221 to 207 BC
> Han Dynasty: 202 BC to AD 220
> T'ang Dynasty: 618 to 906
> Ming Dynasty: 1368 to 1644

You can associate the dynasty to its dates first, then Link the dynasties, or vice versa. I'd Link them first. You can start the Link with a picture of *Dinah* (or a *diner*) drinking *Chinese tea* (*Dinah's Chinese tea* — Chinese dynasties).

Link that to a *prehistoric* animal (coming out of the tea). The prehistoric animal is a *chow* (or it waits on a chow line) to remind you of Chou Dynasty. The chow bites you on the *chin* (Ch'in) and then on the *hand* (Han). Or, you might want to see a hand growing out of your chin. A gigantic hand is in a *tank* (T'ang), or it's saying *thanks*; there's a *mink* (Ming) in the tank.

Any Link using your own words or thoughts will do. Then

associate the dates to your Substitute Words. You'd most likely know which are BC, but if you want a reminder, get *Bic, buck,* or *back* into your picture. *Ad*vertisement would be a reminder for AD, but you don't need reminders for both; one (for either BC or AD) will suffice. Try it on your own.

It's important to know the major wars of world history and the vital dates (or so I'm told by many students). You'd also want to know cause and effect. Knowing that, you can draw logical conclusions about societies politically, economically, socially. The knowledge can tell you a lot about a particular nation before, during, and after the war. Knowing the Substitute Word (or thought) and the phonetic techniques makes it easy to learn the list that follows. These are some of the wars and dates listed in a study guide for high-school and college-history students:

War of Devolution: 1667–1668
Dutch War: 1672–1678
Great Northern War: 1700–1721
War of the Spanish Succession: 1701–1714
War of the Polish Succession: 1733–1736
War of the Austrian Succession: 1740–1748
Seven Years' War: 1756–1763
French Revolutionary and Napoleonic Wars: 1792–1815
Crimean War: 1854–1855 (other sources give 1853–1856)
Austro-Sardinian War: 1859
Danish War: 1864
Franco-Prussian War: 1870–1871

To know them by number, use your Peg Words. For sequence only, Link them. Put the wars in the order you need first; do you want to know them by date, by area of the world, or alphabetically? Assume you want to know them chronologically, as above. Associate each war with the year(s), then Link them.

Devil or *evolution* would remind you of the War of Devolution. Associate *devil* with *dish chalk* to remind you of 1667; if all you need is '67, associate it with *chalk* only. Or, *dish chalk chef* (or **shove**) for 1667–68.

You're going out *dutch* treat with a *coin* (72) to have dinner in a *cave* (78), or **concave**, or *dish coin cave* — for Dutch War, 1672–1678.

Great Northern War, 1700–1721. The *great North* Star is sewing sand (**sew sand** — 00–21; or use **seasoned**). Simply get *tack* (17) into the picture if you need a "century" reminder.

Spanish Succession, 1701–1714. People crossing a *span* (bridge) in *succession* would remind you of the war. If you see those people crossing and sitting on a tire (**sit** *tire* — 01–14), you've got the "year" reminders.

Polish Succession, 1733–1736. Barber *poles* are marching in *succession.*

Connect that to *mummy* or **ma'am** (33) and to *match* (36).

Austrian Succession, 1740–1748. *Horse train* (Austrian) is *succeeding* when it **rows** (40) on a *roof* (48).

Seven Years' War, 1756–1763. A *cow* (7) is fighting with some *ears* (years); the cow is **ticklish** (1756). All you need is the date the war began — obviously.

French Revolutionary and Napoleonic Wars, 1792–1815. See Napoleon (hand in jacket) or a gigantic napoleon pastry fighting with a **dog** *bone* (1792) and a *dove* **tail** (1815). If you don't need the century reminders, **bundle** (92–15) will do.

Crimean War, 1854–1855. Associate *crime* with *lure lily* (54–55). What if your source gives 1853–1856 as the dates for this war? No problem; associate *crime* to **limb leech**.

Austro-Sardinian War, 1859. See a *horse throw*ing (Austro) a *sardine* into a *dove*'s **lap** (1859) — or use **develop**).

Danish War, 1864. A Great *Dane* is sitting in your **chair** (64).

Franco-Prussian War, 1870–1871. A gigantic *frank* is *pressin'* a **casket** (or **kiss cat** — 70–71).

If you've formed the associations and *reviewed* them, you should be able to answer any test questions about these war names and years. If the question is, "When did the Seven Years' War start?" the silly picture of a **ticklish** *cow* fighting some *ears*, tells you that the date is 1756. If you're told the dates in the question, your association will tell you which war it is.

If you want to know the wars in sequence, Link "devil" to "dutch treat" to "great North Star" to "span succession" to "barber poles" to "horse train" and so on. You can put any other important information into your pictures — participants, who won, where the war was fought. It's up to you.

A college student recently showed me this question on one of his history exams: "Identify Uriah Stephens, Haymarket Square, the National Labor Union, Samuel Gompers, the Homestead steel plant, Eugene V. Debs, and the Pullman strike." If you were studying these events, your thinking might proceed something like this:

Uriah Stephens. Founder of Knights of Labor in 1869. Visualize yourself saying, "You're higher" (Uriah) to many hens on a steep hill (steep hens — Stephens). It's at night or you're in armor (Knights) and the hens are busy at their labor (Knights of Labor). See a *ship* laboring with them, if you want to remember the date — 1869.

Haymarket Square. Site in Chicago where a bomb exploded during a Knights of Labor rally, killing eleven people. See hay with escargot (or chick cargo) being sold in a market that's square (Chicago, Haymarket Square); lots of knights (in armor) are laboring in the market, *really* laboring (Knights of Labor rally). A bomb explodes in the market, killing a *tot* or a gigantic **toad** (11 — eleven people were killed).

National Labor Union. William Sylvis created it in 1866; it was the first federation of unions. Picture all the *laborers* in the country (national) joining hands on a train (*choo-choo* — 66); there's a gigantic *bill* (William) on the train — it turns *silver* (Sylvis).

Samuel Gompers. Founder of the American Federation of Labor (1886); he was its president for many years until his death in 1924; the AFL took the place of the Knights of Labor. See a *mule* (Samuel) in *rompers* (Gompers) on a gigantic *fish* (86). The fish waves an *American* flag as it feeds rations (*fed-a-ration*) to *laborers* (American Federation of Labor). Of course, an *ape* (**A**) breaking off *half* (**F**) of an *el* (**L**) would also do. The fish becomes *president* and plays a fiddle like emperor *Nero* (24) supposedly did while Rome burned. All the knights (in armor) are replaced by fish. (AFL replaced Knights of Labor.)

Homestead steel plant. Scene of battle in Homestead, Pennsylvania, between strikers and 300 private guards. Someone is *steal*ing a *home* in*stead* of a *plant* (that manufactures *pens* that are *silly*) while being struck by *private* **masses** (or **muses** — 300).

Eugene V. Debs. Head of American Railway Union; became nationally known during the Pullman Strike; ran for U.S. president five times on Socialist Party ticket. *Debs* (debutantes) is probably enough. But debs eating *veal* (**V**) in *jeans* (Eugene V.) reminds you of the entire name. Perhaps *American* flags are coming out of the debs' heads and getting on trains to join each other (head of American Railway Union). They *pull* a *man* in and *strike* him as the nation watches (nationally known during Pullman Strike). The man runs to the *law* (ran 5 times), but he's caught and forced to *socialize* at a *party*.

Pullman strike. Strike by workers at Pullman's car factory; later joined by American Railway Union members; President Cleveland, on pretext of ensuring the movement of mail, sent troops to preserve order. Visualize men refusing to work as they're pulled (*pull man*) toward the work. See *American* flags coming by *railway* to help. So many *troops* arrive that they *cleave* the *land* (Cleveland); tons of *mail* fall into the "cleaved" land.

I know that if you're studying American or world history, there's an awful lot for you to remember. Learning historical facts is good practice for you even if you're not studying history. Don't worry, there are plenty more subjects coming up!

Chapter 15

Spelling
. . .

Make No Misteak about It! (Dyslexic?)

*C*an you spell "dyslexic"? You *could* visualize a *dean* (**D**) drinking *wine* (**Y**) as he drives around an *ess* curve (**S**), to remind you of the "y" in "dys." You'd *know* the "le"; get *eggs* or *X-ray* (**X**) in there to remind you of the "x" and you'll be able to spell it. (Dyslexic is more or less a catchall term for "learning disabled." The spelling techniques I'll be discussing in this chapter will be a great help to *all* students, whether dyslexic or not.)

When I attended school, no one ever used the word "dyslexic"; I doubt if it existed. No one talked about "learning-disabled" children, either. What we had then were "ungraded" classes. There was, for example, Geography I and Geography II, and the ungraded class. I assume that "ungraded" meant that the teachers didn't know where to place those students. (Many teachers don't know where to place some students today!)

I asked a remedial therapist, Francee Sugar, "How important is memory to learning-disabled or dyslexic students?" Her answer:

It's incredibly important. They may be deficient in the innate ability to store items in their memories, and when they do, they have difficulty retaining it [which is another way of saying, *knowing* it]. We try to help these students — and all students — develop strategies to help them remember details, dates, and many other components of their curricula. Memory is of utmost importance for *any* learning, but is especially important for learning-disabled students. Your systems involve visual trained-memory strategies.

Mark Sicher is a college freshman at this writing. He used my systems throughout high school and uses them now in college to, in his words, "breeze through my courses and exams." He tutored learning-disabled students while still in high school himself. He told me of one boy — let's call him Bill — who seemed totally uninvolved with his work and never made eye contact. Mark demonstrated what could be done with the systems (some show-off stuff) and then taught Bill how to do it. Mark tells me that the change in Bill was amazing and immediate. The self-esteem that resulted was marvelous. Bill's mother called to say that Bill had done his homework that day for the first time in a long time, that there was a new light in his eyes!

Francee Sugar said:

Oh yes. Bill was given a strategy to use on his own. Even if he hadn't applied the systems to all his schoolwork, they would have still been a great help — self-esteem-wise, and to let him see that, yes, he could do it. Your systems gave him a way to feel confident and to do so easily, to enable him to retrieve answers more quickly. For a learning-disabled student, there is good feedback when he can arrive at the right answer, quickly. Exposure to strategies is very important for students. When they know that systems are there and that they do help them remember, their anxieties are relieved and the confidence they absolutely need is available.

Author Jerome Rosner agrees in his book *Helping Children Overcome Learning Difficulties* (Walker and Co., 1979):

Hard-to-teach [learning-disabled] *children are hard to teach because they do not remember enough of what they are taught.* [The italics are his.] You cannot reason effectively unless you can associate information [and] you cannot profit fully from today's lesson unless you can remember yesterday's with relative ease. . . . Without the ability to identify what to remember and *how best to remember it*, school learning is virtually impossible. [I've been saying it — *there is no learning without memory* — since the early 1950s!] Make clear a system — a strategy — that will help the [student] retain information, that is, link up the information he is to learn with the information he already knows.

I'm quite proud of the fact that my systems can also be of help to young people with emotional problems having to do with drugs, alcohol, depression. And they can help, according to Professor Ronald Sobel, a doctor of educational administration who teaches special-education and research-in-education courses to teachers at Adelphi University. He's also a behavior consultant at Island Park School District and coordinator of special-education schools at Hillside Hospital in New York State. (We can assume he knows what he's talking about!)

Professor Sobel himself uses my techniques. He has taught the number system to emotionally disturbed fifth- and sixth-graders (for basics, like the multiplication tables). Mostly, he teaches these young people the Link technique. He tells me that many of them have a "show-me" attitude:

Many of them thought they *couldn't* learn. The various "normal" means simply never worked for them. Well, as I teach them to Link, say, twenty things, they start to pay attention, and when they can do it, their eyes light up — the attitude now is "I *can* learn!" The upward leap in self-esteem is immeasurable.

These kids never could achieve, so they gave up. This kind of frustration led to behavior problems. I believe that, in many cases, when they memorized (learned) a list of items, it changed their lives. I go back into a classroom a week later and there's happy excitement as they show me that they still remember all the items. It's a breakthrough; it gives them some pride, something at which to excel.

Okay. One of the reasons I've included this section is that I want adults (parents, uncles, aunts, friends) to know that the techniques taught here can help learning-disabled and dyslexic students, in *very* positive ways, including the self-esteem area. (I'm aware of the intricacies involved in teaching learning-disabled students and I realize that not all my systems can work for all of them.)

I call it persistence of error. You usually make the same spelling "misteak" every time you spell a particular word. Poor spelling is a memory problem — you don't remember the correct spelling or you remember the *in*correct spelling. You can help yourself to remember most "trap" areas of words you *habitually* misspell by applying the basic rule of memory: **Associate what you want to remember to something you already do know or remember.** I'll give you some examples of that in a moment. But first, let me touch on a way to break that persistence of error, a way to bring that error (which you usually commit unconsciously) into your conscious mind. This is, in other words, a way to *force yourself* to *think* about it.

Most people misspell the word "liquefy"; they spell it "liquify." Let's assume you habitually make that mistake. Break the habit like this: Print the word spelled the *wrong* way on a piece of paper — but print the incorrect letter, the trouble spot, larger than the others: liqu **I** fy. Then, put an X (to show that it's wrong) through that wrong letter: liqu ✗ fy. Do exactly the same thing *five* times. Yes, it sounds silly, but *do* it.

You've made the error *consciously*; you're now aware of that error. Then, lock in the *correct* spelling. Print the word, making the correct letter larger than the others: liqu **E** fy. Circle or underline that correct letter: liqu Ⓔ fy. Do it *five* times.

Do exactly what I've told you and I guarantee you'll never again misspell "liquefy." Doing it the wrong way, as explained, five times has made you conscious of the habitual error. Then, doing it correctly five times is your first step toward making the correct spelling habitual!

Do the same thing with any habitually misspelled words when one letter is the "culprit." The word "separate" is one such. It is often misspelled as "seperate." Do as you just learned. First, "sep ✗ rate," five times; then "sep Ⓐ rate" five times.

Whenever you come across such a word that habitually gives you trouble, apply this idea. You might want to apply it to some of these:

tariff — not tarriff	professor — not proffessor
mortgage — not morgage	exhibition — not exibition
arctic — not artic	receipt — not receit
jewelry — not jewlry	misspell — not mispell

lonely — not lonly   fortunately — not fortunatly
bicycle — not bicicle   actor — not acter
muscle — not mussle   boundary — not boundery

"Calendar" is often misspelled "calender." You can use the idea I just taught you. But because you know the letter words (ape, bean, sea, dean . . .), there's an easier way. Simply visualize an *ape* (which represents the letter **a**) tearing pages from a calendar. That's all — that tells you that an **a** belongs in that "trap" (trouble) area.

If you usually misspell it "insurence," picture an *ape* selling insurance. See an *eel* having a pleasant (or long) existence to remind you that that word is spelled with an **e**. Picture *two hems* shooting **amm**unition at each other to remind you that there are two **m**'s there. See an *ape* getting an allow**a**nce, an *eel* performing surg**e**ry, an *ape* being sep**a**rated.

What a good idea this is! But wait — there's more. Look at this sentence: "Never beLIEve a LIE." A teacher showed that to my class in an early grade. There were a few things that nudged me into my long career as a memory-training specialist, but this was probably the biggest push. I don't think that even the teacher realized that she was applying that basic rule of memory. She was. All the children knew how to spell "lie"; it was the spelling of "believe" that was the problem. Thinking of that sentence, "Never beLIEve a LIE," solved that problem. And I realized that the concept could be used in almost every area of memory.

But staying with spelling for the moment: this specific idea will work for (and against) many tricky words. A "**pie**ce of **pie**" and "**all** lines are parallel," for example. The small word that you already know how to spell (**pie, all**) helps you remember the correct spelling of the longer word. A few more examples:

> You **err** when you int**err**upt.
> **Iron** is part of our envi**ron**ment.
> A cat**a**log advertised **a log** for sale.
> You have an arg**um**ent over **gum**.
> He had a col**oss**al **loss**.
> It's **rough** to get th**rough**.
> She told her sec**ret**ary a **secret**.

We'll be **wed** on a **Wed**nesday.
A **balloon** is shaped like a **ball**.
To **age** is no tr**age**dy.
Don't **eat** l**eat**her.
In F**eb**ruary you say, "**Br**, it's cold."
To balance a **feat**her is a **feat**.
You make a **gain** when you find a bar**gain**.
You **miss** out when you **miss**pell.

When you apply the idea to a word that's been a problem for you, try to really see the "action," the picture or premise, in your mind. Can you apply the technique to any of these?

mis**chief**	deter**mine**	kindergarten	**peas**ant
fr**eight**	**court**esy	ne**cess**ary	**labora**tory
perm**anen**t	illustrate	**tal**ent	**busi**ness
vill**ain**	capa**city**	wi**tch**	min**ute**

Now, another weapon or two. Some tricky words don't fit exactly into the above mold, but the same basic concept works.

"Pres**ence**" is the opposite of abs**ence**; "pres**ents**" are gi**fts**.
You **eat** a "st**eak**"; you kill a sn**ake** with a "st**ake**."
A sove**reign** "**reign**s"; it "**rain**s" water; a rider pulls the "**reins**."
The h**eat** causes bad "w**eat**her" (not "wh**eth**er").
A "coun**cil**" sits; a "coun**sel**" advises.

People often confuse the spelling and the meaning of words that sound exactly the same. "Stationery/stationary" and "principal/principle" are good examples. Look at this:

A "princi**ple**" is a ru**le**.
Your school "princi**pal**" is your "princi**pal**" (main) **pal**.
You use "station**ery**" for a lett**er** (or to writ**e**).
You are "station**ary**" when you st**a**nd (or st**ay**).

Concentrate on these for a minute or so and you'll never confuse them again. You can do the same with other words. Soon you will realize that you don't need both concepts for each word. Concentrating on one of them will serve the purpose. For example, "navel" and "naval." If you think of the "navel" as the belly button, that should do it for you. It isn't necessary also to use "naval"/navy or (water), although you can if you want.

"Capitol" is spelled with an **o** when it refers to the domed building that houses Congress in Washington, D.C., or a building where a state legislature sits. "Capital" with an **a** is how you spell the word for a chief city or the word that refers to money.

> "capit**ol**" — dome
> "capit**al**" — main city of a state or nation; cash

So even if a troublesome word doesn't contain a "helper" word that you already know, you can still use an association technique. If you concentrate for just a moment on the fact that the word "desert" has only one **s** and so does the sand in a desert, you'll know that "desert" is spelled with one **s**. Alternatively, or in addition: "dessert" is eaten after dinner (double letters in each word).

Knowing how to spell one word can help you to remember how to spell another. When a student asked me how to remember whether the word "occasion" is spelled with one **c** or two, I asked him if he knew how to spell the word "accident." The answer was yes, he knew it was spelled with two **c**'s. I suggested thinking of the sentence "On occasion I have accidents." That reminds you that "occasion" is spelled with two **c**'s and just one **s**.

"Alright" is not all right; it's incorrect. "All right" is correct. Just think of *all right* as the opposite of *all wrong*.

Is the spelling of the word "expense" a problem? It is to some; they never know whether it's an **s** or a **c** near the end. Well, visualize this once: **expen$e**. See that dollar sign, which will remind you that it's an **s**.

I've told you how to learn to spell "calendar" correctly. (The bugaboo is that **a** near the end of the word.) Another way would be to see a picture in your mind of either of the following images:

- It's so dark you can't see your "calendar."
- You're throwing darts at your "calendar."

Here are some more examples of how you might apply the techniques to avoid spelling traps:

- There's a lone **e** in "lonely."
- A "flo**w**er" grows; **our** cakes are made with "flo**ur**."
- You usually put a **c**up on a "sau**c**er."
- If you put a **d** in the middle of *with* it gives the word more "wi**d**th."
- The **GM** Company used good "jud**gm**ent" in manufacturing cars.
- There are **eight** pounds in a "w**eight**" (not in a *wait*).
- You "**star**e" at a **star**; "st**air**s" go up in the **air**.
- "Supersede" is the only word with the "-sede" ending. You may have had trouble remembering that **s** because many similar-sounding words are spelled with a **c**: "accede," precede," "secede," and so on. You can use the "print-five-times" method to help you remember the **s**, or you can see a picture of a *super seed*, the kind you plant. That will remind you of the **s**.
- There are lots of "-cede" endings, but only three "-ceed" endings. To remember those, picture this: "In order to *succeed* you have to *proceed* to *exceed*."
- There are quite a few exceptions to the "i-before-e-except-after-c" rule: "counterf**ei**t," "sh**ei**k," "caff**ei**ne," "cod**ei**ne," "prot**ei**n," among others. These and a few other common exceptions can be remembered by learning these sentences: "The counterf**ei**t sh**ei**k thought that caff**ei**ne and cod**ei**ne gave him prot**ei**n." "The w**ei**rd financi**er** s**ei**zes n**ei**ther l**ei**sure nor pleasure."
- Now you know what it **take**s to avoid spelling "mis**take**s."

So you see that you *can* help yourself to remember how to spell correctly. Most any spelling problem can be "handled" by one of the techniques taught in this chapter. Apply these methods and it is impossible for you not to become a better speller than you are now. And bear in mind that the search for the proper technique to apply to a word — the mere attempt to form the association — forces you to concentrate on that word as you never have before. So even if the technique doesn't work — *it works!*

Chapter 16

Law and Politics

• • •

*Remembering and Learning
the Bill of Rights,
Other Amendments,
and Common Law*

You now know just about all you need to know in order to solve any memory problem presented by your schoolwork. All that remains is for you to see just how extensively the techniques can be twisted, altered, and manipulated to do just that. I will be showing you how to apply the ideas to several specific areas of study. (In the next chapter, I'll show you an interesting manipulation of the techniques that can be applied to various fields.) My examples may zero in directly on your current study problems or, as I've already detailed, will show *you* how to zero in on them.

The application discussed in this chapter is valuable in high school and college, and certainly in law school. It's important if you want to learn the first ten amendments to the Constitution of the United States, otherwise known as the Bill of Rights. There are 26 amendments in all, and it's *so* easy to memorize (*know*) them all. You need your first 26 Peg Words, plus one quick association for each. It will take me much longer to write them than it will for you to "see" them.

1. **Freedom of religion, speech, press, and so forth.** A gigantic tie (1) is in church, making a speech; the press is covering the story.

2. **Right to bear arms.** Noah (2) is entering the ark carrying weapons.
3. **Freedom from quartering of soldiers.** Your ma (3) is not allowing soldiers to enter her house.
4. **Guarantee against unreasonable search and seizure.** A gigantic loaf of rye (4) bread is trying to enter your home in order to search and seize (*sneeze,* if you like) it. An American flag stops it from doing so.
5. **Privilege against self-incrimination.** Many policemen (law — 5) are refusing to answer questions in court.
6. **Right to a speedy trial.** A gigantic shoe (6) is rushed in and out of courtrooms (speedily).
7. **Right of trial by jury.** Just picture cows (7) serving as the jury.
8. **Excessive bail and cruel and unusual punishment prohibited.** Somebody is posting bail with a small amount of ivy (8), not with all he has. He's not being punished for it.
9. **People's rights retained.** Gigantic bees (9) are stinging people and pulling off their *right* arms and *retaining* them. (Awful picture — that's why you'll never forget it!)
10. **Residual powers revert to the states.** Visualize toes (10) with large biceps (my standard picture for *power*). The biceps leave and go back to state capitol buildings.

If you've made the associations, you've just learned the Bill of Rights. Go over them; that will show you that you do know them, and it will also be a review. Then, continue.

11. **Exemption of states from suit.** A tot (11) is trying to sue states (capitol buildings) but can't; the states are *exempt from suit.*
12. **Method of electing president and vice president.** Millions of pieces of tin (12) are voting; they all use different *methods.*
13. **Slavery abolished.** A gigantic tomb (13) is whipping its slaves; then it releases them.
14. **Protection of citizen's rights.** Each citizen has a tire (14) around his *right* arm for *protection.*

15. **Right to vote.** A gigantic towel (15) is insisting on its *right* to enter a voting booth.
16. **Income tax.** You're paying your taxes with a dish (16) instead of money. (*That's* a ridiculous picture!)
17. **Election of senators.** Visualize senators each sitting on a tack (17), then jumping up and down and generally carrying on in the Senate. You can, if you like, see an *eel* along with the senators, doing the same *action* (*eel action* — election).
18. **Prohibition.** A gigantic dove (18) is dying for a drink, tries to get one in a bar, and is denied.

This is as good a place as any to stop and mentally review. Review amendments 11 to 18; then mentally review *1 to 18*. Do it before you continue.

19. **Women's suffrage.** Millions of women are in a tub (19) and *voting*.
20. **Abolishment of the "lame-duck" Congress.** Many lame ducks, each with a gigantic nose (20), are ordered out of Congress.
21. **Repeal of prohibition.** A gigantic net (21) is full of whiskey bottles. Everyone grabs one and drinks.
22. **Limit on Presidential terms.** A nun (22) is president of the United States but can't run for office again.
23. **Presidential vote for District of Columbia.** If only "D.C.," or *strict*, would remind you of the amendment, that's all you'd have to associate to name (23). Visualize *DC current*, or a *strict* parent. If not, a column of buses (*column bus* — Columbia) write a name on a ballot. A business card (your *name* is on it) being *strict* could do it for you.
24. **Poll tax abolished.** A fiddle player (Nero — 24) is stopped from collecting money from voters at polls.
25. **Presidential disability and succession.** A gigantic nail (25) takes over as president when the president is disabled, or a gigantic nail disables the president and takes over.
26. **Eighteen-year-old vote.** Young people enter — or **dive** (18)

into — a voting booth and vote by putting a gigantic notch (26) into its wall.

Remember, please, that you're better off thinking up your own silly pictures and associations. That forces Original Awareness, and the pictures *you* come up with are more likely to come back to you when you need them. Mentally review all 26 associations now. You'll see that you know all the amendments! Now a typical law exam question like "Give the rights provided for in the Second, Fourth, and Seventh amendments, specifying the amendment in which each right is contained" will be a cinch for you to answer correctly.

Second, Fourth, and Seventh will make you instantly think of *Noah, rye, cow.* Each of these will bring a thought to mind, a thought that will remind you of the content of the particular amendment. Noah (second) was entering the ark carrying weapons (right to bear arms), and so forth.

Remember that you can put whatever you want into your original association. The First Amendment also contains the right to peaceful assembly and the right to petition the government. You can, if you want to, get *assembly* and *pet itchin'* into that picture.

In *Memory Makes Money,* I showed how lawyers can memorize precedents and discussed how important it is to know those precedents during a trial. I realize that law students have to do the same thing in order to pass their exams (then, after passing those exams, they must use the same techniques to memorize precedents for a trial).

When studying law, you must memorize (learn) statutes and their numbers as well as law precedents. Just a few examples: A New York trial attorney told me that disorderly conduct is penal-law section 240.20. Associate **nears** *nose,* Nero's nose, **nurse nice,** or anything that phonetically represents 240.20 to *disorderly conduct.* (The *nurse* who's usually *nice* is being disorderly.)

The statute defining murder in the second degree is 125.25. See someone committing murder in the second degree (killing a gray beard? Noah — 2) with a gigantic **toenail** and a regular *nail* to remind you of that. If you want to impress your professor by also mentioning the page number on which the information is in the law book, easy enough. If it's on page 396, get **ambush** into your picture and you'll know it.

The same technique works when citing precedents. For example, a well-known case is *Johnson v. Lutz*. This is a precedent regarding the introduction of business records into evidence, which would ordinarily be considered hearsay. You could see a gigantic *john* and its *son* introducing a large *record* (album) to empty *lots* (Lutz) at a *business* meeting. In one of those empty lots is a **new lamb** (volume 253 — the first part of the legal citation) standing on the Empire State Building (for New York — or use *new cork*) having **dinner** (page 124). The dinner is a *mouse* ('30 — 1930). This *tells* you just about all the information you'd need to cite *Johnson v. Lutz* as a legal precedent.

You do not have to associate this kind of information in the same order each time. The order is immaterial; you'll know which association represents which piece of information. I guarantee it.

In 1966, the case of *Miranda v. Arizona* established that persons who are arrested must be informed of their rights; any information obtained from a suspect who has not been properly advised of his or her rights is inadmissible as evidence. Assuming you're familiar with the subject matter, all you need are some reminders. A *veranda* would remind you of Miranda, or you could see a *mirror* on a ve*randa*. *Air zone* (or just *airy* or *owner*) would remind you of Arizona. See yourself floating on air (airy) as you argue a case on a veranda in front of a gigantic *choo-choo* or **judge** (66). You might want to picture a prisoner (man in striped prison suit) being released because he was up in the *air* when he should have been advised of his rights. Incidentally, the Miranda precedent is listed as 384 U.S. 436 (1966). Just associate *veranda* to **mover** to flag (U.S.) to **rematch** to **top judge** or *choo-choo*.

This question appeared on a law exam: "In 1962 a man was tried for a crime and his confession to police was introduced as evidence without his being informed of his right to remain silent. Was the confession admissible evidence?" If you'd memorized the *Miranda v. Arizona* precedent, you'd know that it was established in 1966. So, the answer to the question is "Yes." In 1962, that evidence was still admissible.

One more example, another landmark case. A trial lawyer would cite it this way in court: *"Marbury versus Madison*, one Cranch, one thirty-seven, eighteen oh three." He'd be able to say it that way if he'd made an association between *ma berry* (or *bury*) and *mad at son* (or *medicine*) and *tie* (1) and *crunch* or *ranch* (it's in the *first* volume of the Cranch reporter) and **atomic** (page 137) and *dove* **sum** (the year 1803). And it would have taken no time at all to make or see that association.

As mentioned before, the techniques taught here to use for schoolwork and for passing exams will "roll over" into your professional life. I'm helping you jump the gun. For example, in *Memory Makes Money*, I wrote:

> Herald Price Fahringer is one of the best-known trial attorneys in New York. He defended socialite Claus von Bulow during the first of von Bulow's widely publicized murder trials. In Fahringer's opinion, jury selection is the most important part of a criminal trial. In an article on this subject in the *New York Law Journal*, he lists the "topics of inquiry" that an attorney should know and pursue in order "to gain the necessary knowledge to make an enlightened choice." He talks of having a written list but adds: "On the other hand, to be effective . . . counsel should try to avoid the use of notes. Being 'pad bound' is distracting. A good trial lawyer wants to establish a great deal of eye contact with the jurors." Fahringer then suggests employing my *Link System*. He uses it.

So you see that what you're learning here is extremely important for your schoolwork, but will be just as important in your professional or business career.

Chapter 17

Memorize Graphic Materials
• • •
Maps and Locations, the Periodic Table, Atomic Numbers, and More

*W*ouldn't it be a great help for school study if you could easily memorize locations of places on maps? Locations of *anything* on graphs, charts, layouts, and so forth? Well, you can! And memorizing the locations will, at the same time, make it easier for you to remember the actual items, places, and information at those locations. I want to teach you a technique — actually, a *strategy* — about which I'm pleased and proud. It's called the *Memory Graph*. I devised it back in the 1950s when I was asked to help a postal employee remember the locations (and, in those days, *zone* numbers) of streets in his city. When a student asked me more recently to help her memorize the map location of all fifty states, I applied the strategy — and it was *perfect*. (I'll teach you another fascinating application of the Memory Graph in this chapter.)

You *could* form anywhere from six to nine separate Links of the states, moving roughly from west to east, and from north to south, or vice versa. For example, moving eastward, your first Link might be Alaska (baked *Alaska*) to Washington (*washing*) to Oregon (*oar gone*) to California (*call a fawn*) to Hawaii (*how are ya'*). The next Link could start with Montana (*mountain Anna*) and move southward to New Mexico (*new sombrero*). This idea *will* help; it *will* work.

But the Memory Graph is a much better way to do it. The same technique can be used for any information that's laid out on graphs or tables. Look at the graph at the bottom of this page.

What I've done here is to break the country into nine sections the way *I* would want to learn the state locations (you would lay your graph out the way *you* would want to learn them): Northwest (A1), West (B1), Southwest (C1), North Central (A2), Central (B2), South Central (C2), Northeast (A3), East (B3), and Southeast (C3). The simple idea is that you invent a specific *pigeonhole* for each region and "lock" the states of that section into it. You'll need *nine* such pigeonholes. Just make up a word that will *specifically and definitely* represent each section. The words must be easy to remember. They will be, they are — because you know the Phonetic Number/Alphabet. Each word will *start with the vital letter* and will end with the *consonant sound that represents the number.* That will be your pigeonhole.

The word for A1 is *ate* — what else? It begins with **A** and the next (and only) consonant sound is **T**, which can represent *only* 1. So *ate* can represent *only* A1. No decisions to make. The word for A2 must begin with **A** and the only consonant sound must be **N**,

	1	2	3
A	Alaska Montana Washington Idaho Oregon Wyoming	No. Dakota Wisconsin So. Dakota Michigan Minnesota Indiana	Maine Massachuset New Hampshire Connecticut Vermont Rhode Island New York Pennsylvania New Jersey
B	California Utah Nevada Colorado	Nebraska Missouri Kansas Illinois Iowa	Maryland Virginia Delaware Kentucky Ohio Tennessee West Virginia No. Carolina
C	California New Mexico Arizona Hawaii	Texas Arkansas Oklahoma Louisiana	So. Carolina Alabama Mississippi Georgia Florida

for 2. The word I use is *awn* (a sunshade). The pigeonhole for A3 is *aim*: it begins with **A** and the consonant sound is **M** for 3. And —

B1 = bat   C1 = cat
B2 = bean   C2 = can
B3 = bomb   C3 = comb

Go over them two or three times; that's all that's necessary. Some of the words are the same as other Peg Words you may be using, but it doesn't matter. They work separately and well for this specific technique. You'll see that this is so when you actually try it. You can, of course, always change words — as long as they fit into the pattern I've devised.

Now, how do you use them? Easy. Link all the states in section A1 to *ate*, that's all. There are two ways to go. You can start with the section word and Link all the Substitute Words for the states in that section to it. You'd start with *ate*, for example, and associate that to Alaska, Washington, Oregon, Montana, Idaho, Wyoming. Or, you can associate *ate* (eating) to Alaska, then associate *ate* to Washington, *ate* to Oregon, *ate* to Montana, and so on. You have to decide which is better for you — by trying both ways. So, for section B1, associate *bat* to California, then continue the Link, or associate *bat* to each state in that section, separately. Do that for each section. When you've made your Links/associations, you'll not only know all the states, you'll know their locations!

If you need to be reminded of, say, the South Central states, visualize the Memory Graph; you'll know that the South Central states are pigeonholed in C2, and that will automatically make you think of *can*, and *can* will tell you the states in that area.

Do you need to know where Nebraska is located? You may have used *new brass car* as the substitute phrase, and you associated it to *bean*; or, it's in the Link that starts with *bean*. (You might have pictured a new brass car completely full of beans.) This tells you that Nebraska is in section B2, and that tells you that Nebraska is one of the Central states.

Visualize the silly picture of you *carry*ing a *line* (Carolina) of *bomb*s (B3) in a storm (*storm* is my standard picture for *north*, because north makes me think of cold and, therefore, storms).

That tells you that North Carolina is part of the Eastern section of the country. Make up your own standard picture for "north," of course; shaking your head no would do it if you decided that it represents "no.," the abbreviation for north. Or *moth* — it sounds like "north."

Remember, you can list the states any way you want to and Link them in any order you like. Always do what's best for *you*. If you feel that you'd like to pinpoint the locations a bit more, you can enlarge the Memory Graph to a four-by-four format; that is, add a "4" column down and a "D" row across. (You'll see how the graph can be enlarged in a moment.) On the other hand, for some memory problems, you might need only four sections (A1, A2, B1, B2). Your choice. I've included California in two sections of this graph; this is to remind me that California is a long state and is part of both the West and Southwest.

I just want you to realize that you can superimpose the map of any country or region onto a Memory Graph and form your own associations. Use your imagination and you'll find many uses for the graph that can be useful to you.

Learning the capitals of the states is a simple matter. Associate your Substitute Word for the state to your Substitute Word for the capital city. For instance, *mixing* something *again* (mix again — Michigan) and something *lands singing* (Lansing) into the mixture.

Obviously, you can apply that technique to any country in the world. If you picture a kangaroo (to remind you of Australia) eating a *can* of *berries*, it will remind you that Canberra is the capital of Australia. A seemingly tough one: The capital of Honduras is Tegucigalpa. *Under ass, hand duress, hand a dress* (to someone), or a *Honda* car would all remind you of Honduras. Associate one of them to *take you* (to) *see gulper* (one who gulps). Perhaps, you *hand a dress* to someone, and say, "Put it on and I'll *take you* to *see gulper*." It's no longer a tough one!

Do you want to know the rivers of a country? Form Substitute Words for their names and Link them in the order that would remind you of general location. You can even include the names of the cities through which they flow. Just start your Link with the name of a river; Link the other rivers, and the cities, to that.

A Link of the seven continents in size order might be: *a chair* (Asia) to *a free car* (Africa) to *a merry car* in a storm (north; or just an American flag in a storm — North America) to another *merry car* with a big *mouth* (South America) to an *ant* doing *artwork* in a car (Antarctica) to *you rope* (Europe) to *ass trail ya* or to a kangaroo (Australia).

Now, here's a strange segue — I'm taking you from states, countries, maps to *chemistry*. Oh, chemistry memory problems will be discussed again, later. Right now, I want to show you how the Memory Graph can help you learn one of the difficult-to-remember concepts in that subject. People have told me that they have needed to know the periodic table in high school, in college, and in graduate school and beyond, but that they never did quite "get it." It's not at all difficult to "get" if you apply the following idea using the Memory Graph. The first thing you have to do is to compare the periodic table in your chemistry textbook to this one:

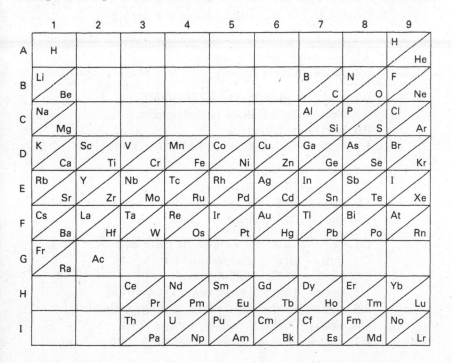

I've condensed by placing symbols for *two* elements into all the occupied "pigeonholes" except A1 and G2. If you wanted to draw the periodic table, you'd take the two elements I've shown in single squares and place them in separate squares arranged "left/right" of each other.

You could, of course, simply form separate Links for each row or column — making up words and pictures to remind you of the symbols. I've found the Memory Graph to be the easiest way. You already know the pigeonhole words for A1 to A3, B1 to B3, and C1 to C3. I'll give you all the other words; go over them two or three times and you'll know them. In a short while, you won't be able to forget them even if you wanted to!

For most, the word ends with the vital consonant sound, but there is an exception or two. For E3, the word is **em**peror. It's the consonant sound that immediately follows the vital letter that we're interested in, so just ignore any consonant sounds that come after that. Another exception is I9; since **Y** is not used here, you know that *yipe* could only represent I9. All right; here are the pigeonhole words, the symbols for the elements, and a suggestion or two for words to use as reminders of the symbols.

A1, ate — (H) itch, or ache
A9, ape — (H/He) age he

B1, bat — (Li/Be) **liberty**, or **live bed**
B7, bug — (B/C) Before Christ, or **Bic**
B8, buff — (N/O) no
B9, baby — (F/Ne) **fine**, or half knee, or fanny

C1, cat — (Na/Mg) nay mug
C7, coke — (Al/Si) Al, *si* (yes)
C8, cave — (P/S) PS (postscript), or **pose**
C9, cap — (Cl/Ar) **clear**, or Clara

D1, dot — (K/Ca) cane **cave**, or cane **cake**
D2, den — (Sc/Ti) scat eye, or sic Ty
D3, dam — (V/Cr) VCR or **vicar**
D4, deer — (Mn/Fe) **man fee**, or **my knife**
D5, doll — (Co/Ni) **cold night**, or Coney (Island)
D6, dash — (Cu/Zn) cousin, or cue zone
D7, dog — (Ga/Ge) gage, or Georgia, gee

D8, dive — (As/Se) **asse**t, or ass see
D9, dope — (Br/Kr) broker

E1, eddy (a "whirlpool") — (Rb/Sr) rib sore, or robe sir
E2, enter — (Y/Zr) wine zero, or yezzir (yes sir)
E3, emperor — (Nb/Mo) nab Moe
E4, err — (Tc/Ru) **tack Ru**th, or tic rude
E5, eel — (Rh/Pd) blood police department (or **paid**), or **red
    ho**t PD
E6, edge — (Ag/Cd) age cod (or cad, or **c**ertificate of
        deposit)
E7, egg — (In/Sn) in sun, or insane
E8, eve — (Sb/Te) sub tea (or team)
E9, ebb — (I/Xe) eye (or I) **X**erox

F1, fat — (Cs/Ba) Casbah
F2, fun — (La/Hf) **lauhf**(gh), or lay half, or lay hi-fi
F3, foam — (Ta/W) Taiwan, or tawny, or ta-ta Waterloo
F4, fur — (Re/Os) **Renos**, or **re: O**scar
F5, foil — (Ir/Pt) iron pot, or irk pit
F6, fish — (Au/Hg) hey you hag (or hog), or **au**tumn **hog**
F7, fake — (Tl/Pb) tall pub
F8, fife — (Bi/Po) bipole, or **big po**le
F9, fib — (At/Rn) **a train**, or **a turn**, or **at** Registered Nurse, or
    a tea run

G1, gat — (Fr/Ra) fire ray, or furry rat
G2, gown — (Ac) **ace**, or **act**, or AC current

H3, ham — (Ce/Pr) **ice prongs**, or **cent per**
H4, hare — (Nd/Pm) nod poem, or nod PM, or nude Pam
H5, hill — (Sm/Eu) small ewe, or some eulogy, or Sam
        Europe
H6, hash — (Gd/Tb) good Tab, or God TB
H7, hog — (Dy/Ho) dye hole, or dean wine **ho**me
H8, hive — (Er/Tm) error team, or ear time
H9, hop — (Yb/Lu) wine **blue**, or **you bet Lu**cy

I3, I'm — (Th/Pa) the Pa
I4, ire — (U/Np) UN pea, or you nap
I5, ill — (Pu/Am) pew AM, or peeyoo in the morning
I6, itch — (Cm/Bk) come back
I7, icky — (Cf/Es) café espresso, or cafés
I8, ivy — (Fm/Md) FM doctor, or **fa**mous doctor, or **fame mad**
I9, (y)ipe — (No/Lr) no lair, or no liar

It's all clear after you go over it a couple of times. The symbol reminders I've listed are the first ones that came to my mind, the ones I would use. They needn't be exact, they just have to *remind* you. You can use the letter words more often than I have. An example: For H5 (Sm/Eu), you could see an ess curve (**S**) with a hem (**m**) driving on it, going up a hill (H5); an eel (**E**) and a ewe (**u**) are sewing the hem. That's fine; I prefer the kind of reminders I've listed. A funeral on a hill, and the eulogy going on and on, which makes me think, "Some eulogy," gives me the information I need. *Aw heck* associated to fish (F6) would remind me that Au and Hg belong there, even though the phrase contains different letters.

It's all so simple: a *fat* (F1) man walking in the Casbah (Cs/Ba); a *dog* (D7) arrives in Georgia and says, "Georgia, gee!" (Ga/Ge); you go into a few cafés (Cf/Es) and they're all *icky* (I7) — these pictures must remind you of the information you want. If you know the full name of the element, you can use a Substitute Word for that, if you prefer.

After you've made your associations and mentally reviewed them, lay out a nine-by-nine graph (or picture one in your mind) and think of each pigeonhole word. Think of E5 (eel) and it tells you that Rh and Pd belong there. D5 (doll) tells you that Co and Ni go directly above Rh and Pd. If rows H and I are not important to you, omit them; then your graph need only include boxes A1 to G2. I've given you the pigeonhole words only for the *occupied* squares, but as you've seen, it's easy to make up the other words when you need them.

Maybe you'd rather not double up the symbols in column 1 or column 9. The graph can be expanded to ten or eleven (or more) columns; lay it out whichever way is best for you. If you need pigeonhole words for squares A10 and A11 through I10 and I11, follow the pattern. Use the **S** sound (for the zero) to remind you of column 10: *ace* for A10; *base* for B10; and so on. For A11, you could use *added*; B11 — *baited*; C11 — *coated*, or *cadet*; D11 — *dated*; E11 — *edit*; F11 — *feted*, or *faded*; H11 — *hated*; I11 — *I did*, or *I died*.

Students have learned the periodic table in about half an hour using this technique! And you can put any other information into your original associations. The atomic numbers for yttrium (Y) and zirconium (Zr) are, respectively, 39 and 40. Get **moppers** into your *enter* (E2) pigeonhole and you'll "have" that information also. Actually, all you need is one number for each pair because the elements in each square have ascending atomic numbers. So, only mop (39) is needed in E2; you'd know that the atomic number for the other element is 40.

Learn — understand — the Memory Graph. It may become one of the most useful weapons in your arsenal for fighting forgetfulness.

Chapter 18

Music

• • •

*Notes, Compositions,
and Composers*

$\mathcal{T}$here's a cliché among music teachers: "rote to note." It refers to the boredom of rote-to-note memorizing that has caused many students to give up on studying music before it starts to be fun. I don't know much about music, but I can discuss the memory problems that beginners in music have described for me. I've mentioned "Every Good Boy Does Fine" to help remember/know the lines of the treble clef (EGBDF). For the spaces, there's FACE. Students can use the same idea to lock in quickly the lines and spaces of the bass clef: GBDFA and ACEG — "Good Boys Do Fine Always" and "All Cars Eat Gas."

I've been told that *key signatures* are fundamental, both for reading and understanding music and for playing an instrument. Knowing key signatures is certainly basic when studying music theory. I'll talk mainly about sharps (♯), and you can apply the idea to flats (♭) yourself; I'll just touch on them. (The key signature is the configuration of sharps or flats placed after a clef to indicate the specific key.)

Look at this chart:

C	G	D	A	E	B	F♯	C♯
↕	↕	↕	↕	↕	↕	↕	↕
0	1	2	3	4	5	6	7

A sheet of music often has sharp (or flat) signs at the top after the treble clef. The number of sharp signs you see tells you the key for that piece of music. And the chart above shows you *how many* sharps there are for each major key. (All memory problems break down to entities of two, eventually. This is a good example. For this specific problem, you need know only two things — the name of the key and the number of sharps it has.)

There are three sharp signs here:

The chart above tells you that three sharps is the key of A major. To know this quickly, use the technique I taught you for forming the Memory Graph pigeonhole words; it fits perfectly. Just make up a word that starts with the letter (the name of the key) and that is followed by the consonant sound that tells you the number of sharps in that key. *"Cuss, gut, den, aim, err, bull, fudge,* and *cook"* would do admirably. There's no need to Link these words to each other, just as there was no need to Link the Memory Graph words. Just think of them for a short time and you'll know these key signatures. Then, when you see five sharp signs, you'll think of the sound for 5 (L), which will remind you of the word that ends with that sound (*bull*), which begins with **B** — B major!

In the key of C major, the seven basic notes of the musical scale (in sequence) are CDEFGAB. When I first heard this many years ago, I thought, *"See* the *deaf* (person) *gab."* The letter **C** made me think of "see," and that in turn would *remind* me of the note C, "deaf" of DEF, and "gab" of GAB. It was a spur-of-the-moment association that has proven itself over 40 years! You can, of course, Link the appropriate letter words from chapter 13 — *sea* to *dean* to *eel,* and so on — in order to remember the notes in the C scale.

Remembering *where* a specific note is located on the piano

keyboard is a harder memory problem when you start studying. I assume that's so, or aids like this wouldn't have been devised:

> All the G and A keys
> Are between the black threes
> And 'tween the twos are all the D's;
> Then on the right side of the threes
> Will be found the B's and C's;
> But on the left side of the threes
> Are all the F's and all the E's.

The problem becomes easier to solve if you number the keys. Look:

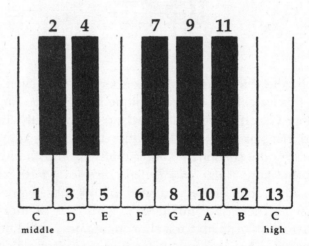

I didn't use the letter words or the Peg Words for the key signatures because I wanted to keep them "clear" for this. Simply associate the letter word for each white note to the Peg Word for the number. Do it and you'll know which key to hit for which note. It's so easy: See your ma (3) kicking the dean (D) of a college and you'll know that D is the white key numbered 3 in the drawing. See an ape (A) with toes (10) all over it to tell you that A is the white key numbered 10, and so on. Do it for all the white keys and you'll know them in no time. Before you know it, the numbers will no longer be necessary and they and the silly pictures will simply fade.

You can also use those numbers to help you remember chords.

Play keys 1, 5, and 8 to get a C chord. Visualize a gigantic **tea leaf** (1, 5, 8) on the *sea* (C) and you've got it. Again, once you do know the positions of the notes, there's no longer a need for the numbers — and that's good; it's the *chords* you want to know. To create a C chord, all you have to know is to play C, E, and G. An F chord is FAC. Some chords require sharp notes (the black keys just to the right of the white ones). Make up a standard picture to remind you of that — "sharp" (a *knife* or *cutting*) will do. The seven basic major chords are listed below, plus the way I would learn them.

C chord — CEG; just picturing a *keg* would do it for me. Or, associate *sea* to **egg**.

D chord — DF♯A; a *dean* holds *half* (F) a *knife* (♯) and fights an *ape* (A).

E chord — EG♯B; Link *eel* to *jeans* cut by a *knife* to *bean*. Or, an **egg** is being *cut* (♯) by a *bean*.

F chord — FAC; just visualize *half* a **face**; or *half* an *ape* goes into the *sea*.

G chord — GBD; **good-bye** *dean*, or a pair of *jeans* go **bad**.

A chord — AC♯E; an *ape* jumps into a *sea* full of *knives* (♯) to catch an *eel*; or an **ace** with a *knife* cuts an *eel*.

B chord — BD♯F♯; a **bed** is being *cut* by *half* a *knife*.

Students have also told me about the problem of memorizing chord progressions. Well, now that you see that you can picture or visualize a chord, you also know that you can Link any number of them in order to remember a progression (sequence) of chords.

Part of music-history courses is the study of composers, their compositions, patrons, and periods, and the kinds of pieces they produced. "Study of" is a definite synonym for *remembering*; apply what you've learned in this book and you'll know what you need to know faster and better than anyone in your class. If you want to remember that Mozart, Salieri, Haydn, and DePonte are composers of the classical period, simply use *class* as a "heading" and form a Link: *class* to *Moe's art* to *sale airy* (or *salary*) to *hay den* (or *hidin'*) to *the pond* (or *D pound E*). Haydn's patron was Prince

Nikolaus Esterházy. Associate *hay den* to *prints* (if you think it necessary) to *nickels* (or *nickel louse*) to *a stair hazy*.

Haydn composed the "Surprise Symphony." Associate your Substitute Word for that to your Substitute Word for Haydn; perhaps you're *surprised* to find *hay* all over your *den*. Rossini composed "The Barber of Seville"; see a *rose* having its hair cut by a *barber* in the *village*. (Or, just see a *rosy barber*.) "The Barber of Seville" is a bel canto opera; get a *bell* into your picture.

Verdi wrote the opera "Falstaff." See yourself asking *"where D?"* of a *staff*, and it *falls*. Tchaikovsky wrote "Swan Lake" and "The Sleeping Beauty." See a *shy cow ski* on a *lake* with many *swans*; the most *beautiful* swan is *sleeping*. Visualize some swans doing *ballet* on the water to remind you that these are ballets. Wagner wrote "Lohengrin"; associate *wag knee* (or *wagon, ah*) to *low N grin*. You can get a Substitute Word (make up a standard) for *opera* into the picture to tell you the kind of piece it is. Wagner's patron was King Ludwig of Bavaria: *crown* (for king), *lead wig, buff area*. Form a good, strong association between *Moe's art* and *down gee van knee* and you'll always know that Mozart wrote "Don Giovanni." To remind you that Leonard (*lean hard*) Bernstein wrote "Age of Anxiety," see someone *burn* a beer *stein*, which causes you so much *anxiety* that you *age*. Get your standard Substitute Word for *symphony* into the picture to tell you that that's what it is.

Associate *straw win ski* (or *drive and ski*) with *pet rush car* and you'll know that Stravinsky composed "Petrouchka." Associate a *bird* on *fire* to *straw win ski* and *write off spring* to *straw win ski* — or "do" both in a single picture — to tell you that Stravinsky also composed "The Firebird" and "The Rite of Spring."

A *violin*, acting as a *con*, sits on a *chair* and steals a *shiny* iceberg; this will remind you that Schoenberg composed a violin concerto.

Debussy composed "La Mer." See a *D* being *busy* with — or *bossy* to (*D bossy*) — a *llama* (or use the sea, if you know that that's what *la mer* means in French).

The systems can be applied to almost any musical memory problem. Apply them to what you want to, the *way* you want to, and you'll be "studying/remembering smart."

Chapter 19

Formulas

• • •

Mathematics, General Science,
Chemistry, Earth Science,
Atomic Numbers, and More

*M*ost of the students I speak with tell me that they'd like to learn to remember *numbers* more than anything else, and remember them faster, better, and more easily. Almost every subject you study throughout your school years entails some number memorizing. When you were in your early grades, you had to memorize the multiplication tables. That's the *only* way to know them, and I'm sure you still know them. Had you been able to apply the Phonetic Number/Alphabet then, it would have been a snap to memorize the "times table" — as it is for young students who use the method now. All that's necessary is that you form an association between problem and solution. A picture of **cuff lash**, for example, would tell you that 7×8 is 56; *ship* to *lure* tells you that 6×9 is 54; *roof* to **man**, that 4×8 is 32.

You most likely don't need this now (you may want to teach it to a younger brother or sister), but there are plenty of other areas in which you can apply it. I can't touch on all of them. I've already touched on some, and I'll touch on a few more now.

In math and science, you're expected to know metric measurements and equivalents. It's so easy. Assume you want to remember (*know*) that .03937 inches equals one millimeter. Form an association between *Milly* (or *mill* of *meters*) and **sum up mug**; if you feel you need a reminder for "inch," get *inch*worm or *p*inch into your picture. A mile is 1.609 kilometers; *smile to* **touches up to** *key low* would do it.

One pound is 453.6 grams. See yourself *pound*ing a **real** *match* (4536) while a *gram*ophone (or your *gram*ma) plays. (You can round it off and use **roller** instead.) A gigantic *key* bent *low* over a *meter* (or *meet her* — kilometer) acting like a **janitor** (6214) with a *smile* (mile) tells you that a kilometer is .6214 of a mile. I haven't bothered with the decimal points because I assume you know where they belong, but you can make any association as specific as you like. Make up a standard Substitute Word for the decimal point (anything with a point, or a pointer) and include that in your picture at the proper place.

For geology or earth science, you should know that the planet Earth's equatorial diameter is roughly 7,927 miles. Just see a **gaping** hole in the earth and millions of *dimes* (for *diam*eter) fall into it.

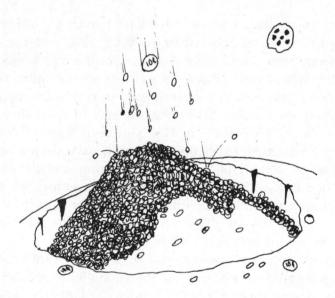

That's *all* you have to do. The Earth's circumference at the equator is about 24,902.45 miles. You might see *Nero* putting **poison** in a *roll* (*Nero poison roll*: 24,902.45) at a *circus conference* (circumference). Again, that's *all*. Earth's average distance from the sun is 92.9 million miles. See a **pinup** girl traveling (or you're sending a *bone*

up) to the sun from Earth. (More on planets later.) The speed of sound in air is 742 miles per hour; a **crown** (or **crane**) travels through the air making strange *sounds*. See a white *fish* (186) having **no fun** (282) in a *light* bulb and you'll know that the speed of light is 186,282 miles per second. Yes, you can put a word for "second" (*sickened?*) in there if you need it.

You're simply connecting concrete images — Substitute Words and phonetic words — to remind you of the necessary information. It works for any subject. For chemistry, you may want to learn all the elements, their symbols, atomic numbers, and atomic weights. Form all your associations in that order.

Iron	Fe	26	55.85
Tantalum	Ta	73	180.95

A short Link for each does it. *I run* to *fee* to *notch* to *lily* **fall**; *tan tall* (or *tan tail* or *tantalize*) to *ta-ta* to *comb* to **doves pull** (or **pail**). This technique turns a major memory/learning problem into an easy game to play. It even works for rules or definitions! The lanthanide series is a series of elements with atomic numbers from 57 to 71. Perhaps you *land at night* (enough to remind you of lanthanide) and you point and say, "**Look, a cat.**" *Tan hide* (or *land and hide*) to **lake** *cot* gives you the same information.

More chemistry later. Now let's see how well the techniques work for mathematical formulas (or any other kind). The formula for finding the area of a circle is "$A = \pi r^2$." You know that "r" stands for radius. I originally learned this by picturing *a round pie iron*. "Round" reminded me of circle (*circus* would also do). *A pie iron* breaks down like this: *A* is A (for area); *pie* is pi. **Iron** reminds me of r^2. It's simple and instantaneous: A round pie is made of iron (you can see yourself hitting it and it clangs like iron). *A circle of fire around Noah* would work for this formula. The "fi" sound in *fire* is enough to remind of pi; the "r" sound is *r* (for radius). *Noah* is 2.

To find the area of a triangle, use the formula "$A = \frac{1}{2}BH$." I originally saw a lamb *try*ing to make *a half bah. Try a half bah. Try* reminds of *triangle*; *a* is area, *half* is $\frac{1}{2}$, of course, and **bah** reminds of BH (base times height). Using the letter words: *half* a *bean itch*ing would do it. To remember "F = MA" (force equals mass times acceleration), see yourself *forc*ing your *ma* to do something.

Well, applying the technique to simple formulas like this is easy and kind of obvious. What about more complicated formulas? Here's the formula for finding the area of a regular polygon:

$$\frac{1}{4} NL^2 \cot \frac{180}{N}$$

All the ideas you've learned come into play here. You'll form a Link of items or actions representing numbers, letters, and words. Always start your Link with a Substitute Word that tells you *what* the Link represents. For this formula, perhaps a *polly* (parrot) is *gone*, lost in a large *area*. That's what I pictured, then the polly turned into a *quarter* (the coin: $\frac{1}{4}$); the quarter was kneelin' (NL^2) — I pictured it kneelin' and looking up to remind me that the ^{2} is *up*, but kneelin' on a *square* (squared) *cot* (cotangent) near a *hen* (N) will also do. The hen is being attacked from *above* (over) by **doves** (180).

It takes very little time to form this Link.

Bear in mind that I'm using the Substitute Words that come to *me*. A *quarter* and *above* are my standards for $\frac{1}{4}$ and "over." Instead of "over," you can use a word that means "divided by" to you. Use what works for *you*. Standards will evolve for you automatically. I always see an American flag to represent the equal (−) sign. (All Americans are *equal*.) I see either a *miner* or a *mynah* bird for "minus," and ap*plause* or a *cross* for "plus." A *tree* means "square *root*" to me.

Say you want to know this formula for harmonic motion:

$$T = 2\pi \frac{\sqrt{M}}{K}$$

"Link" along with me: A *harmonica* is *moving* (harmonic motion) and drinking *tea* (T); the tea is waving an American flag (you usually know where the equals sign goes; if so, don't bother with the reminder; no need to associate things you *know*). *Two pies* (2π) are waving a flag.

Pies are growing on a *tree* (square root); the tree is driving a Mack truck (the *Mack* truck reminds me of M over K). Or, see the truck driving *over* the tree, or associate tree with *hem* (M) *on* a *cake* (K). If you formed the suggested Link, you'd think of harmonic motion and that would make you think of tea (T). Tea makes you think of American flag (=) and flag leads you to two pies (2π). Pies remind you of tree (square root) and that makes you think of Mack (M over K). Associate a *pie* to **mightier** *dish* and you'll know that π equals 3.1416.

The point, as usual, is that now you have tangible things to picture in your mind in order to form a Link that, in turn, *reminds* you of a formula or equation. The system makes the intangible *tangible* and meaningful. And, it **forces you to concentrate** on that formula without even realizing it!

Here are five different kinds of formulas — just for practice. I'll get to more difficult ones soon enough. Meanwhile, try to learn these:

$$\text{Quadratic formula:} \quad x = \frac{-b \pm \sqrt{b^2 - 4ac}}{2a}$$

Start with *aquatic* or *quad*ruplets in an *attic*. Link that to *eggs* (x) waving a flag ($=$); a *miner* ($-$) waves a flag; a *bean* (b) flies out of the miner's head as another miner *applauds over* ($\pm$) it; the applauding miner climbs a *tree* (square root) and goes into a *bin* (b^2); a *mynah* bird ($-$) flies out of the bin with a clothes *rack* (4ac; true memory will tell you that *rack* means 4ac, not Rac or 47) *over* Noah (2) who is wrestling an *ape* (a). There are other choices, of course; this is how I did it. It will only seem complicated if you don't actually try it.

$$\text{Total-energy formula:} \quad E = \frac{-M(\pi K Q_1 Q_2)^2}{N^2 h^2}$$

If you need a reminder for parentheses, you can use *bowlegs*; for "times," the *New York Times* or *dimes*. Another way to be reminded of "over" is to use a *ladder*. Link *energetic eel* to *flag* (and *ladder*; or put *ladder* at the end of that part of the Link that's above the line) to *miner* to *hem* (you can see bowlegs coming out of the dress hem) to *pike* (πK) to *quit* (Q_1) to *queen* (Q_2) with bowlegs, if you feel it's necessary, to *Noah* (or no or new, or to a boxing ring to remind you of "squared,") *over* (or *ladder*) to *noon* (N^2) to *hen* (h^2). Remember, you must *see* the pictures. Try it.

Electric-charge formula: $Q = 6.25 \times 10^{-18}$ charges =
1 coulomb

The words you might use: *cue, flag,* **channel,** *dimes* (for "times,"
only if you think you need it), **tossed off** (include *miner* if you need
to be reminded of "minus"), *charges, flag, tie, column.* The pictures
might be a *cue* stick gets an *electrical charge* and waves a *flag;* a
gigantic *flag* crosses the English *channel;* many *dimes* cross, too,
because they've been *tossed off* into the channel; *charges* of electric-
ity fly out of the dimes; these charges destroy many *flags;* the flags
are made into a huge *tie;* the tie forms a gigantic *column.*

One of the formulas for a form of alcohol is:

1,1 diphenyl 2,2 dimethyl 1,2 ethanediol

Try this: As a *tot* (1,1) *died,* he *fanned* a large letter *L* (*die fan
L* — diphenyl); a *nun* (2,2) also fans the L; the nun gives a *dime* to
Ethel (*dime Ethel* — dimethyl); Ethel can't hold the dime because it
weighs a *ton* (1,2), so she *et* (ate) it as she *aims* at an *old* man who
dies (*et aim die old* — ethanediol; or use *attain dial*). See the pictures
and you'll know this formula.

You can make up a picture for *any* component that appears in a
formula. For delta (Δ), *dealt* (cards); for vector ($\rightarrow$), an arrow; for
reversible reaction ($\rightleftharpoons$), two halves of an arrow; and so on.

One teacher I know gives her class a memory aid for the
formulas needed to find certain trigonometric ratios. The mne-
monic is the nonsense word *sohcahtoa.* These are the formulas:

$$\sin = \frac{\text{opposite}}{\text{hypotenuse}} \qquad \cos = \frac{\text{adjacent}}{\text{hypotenuse}} \qquad \tan = \frac{\text{opposite}}{\text{adjacent}}$$

Do you see how *sohcahtoa* can be a memory aid? The problem is
to remember the word! Well, *soak a toe, so car tow,* or *soak ah toe* all
make sense, can be pictured, and will remind you of that nonsense
word. You're probably better off forming a definite picture for

each formula. For example, a *sign* (sine) is *opposite* a *high pot in use*. A *coat signs* (cosine) as it stands *adjacent* to a *pot*; a *tan gent* (tangent) is tanning his *opposite* side with a lamp that *a J sent*.

Amazing, isn't it? You can memorize formulas easily. Oh, you think the formulas in this chapter were easy ones, and that's the only reason why the techniques worked? I'll take care of *that* notion in the next chapter!

Chapter 20

More Formulas

• • •

Algebraic, Chemical, and Structural Formulas; Molecular Compositions; Electronic Dot Diagrams

"**W**e usually think of mathematics as reasoning, as proving statements that will be used to solve problems," according to Looy Simonoff, associate professor of mathematics at the University of Nevada in Las Vegas.

You can't prove all the statements; you have to *start* with some. Otherwise you'd never get anywhere. The ones you start with, the so-called axioms or first principles, you have to remember. Again, you have to start somewhere, with things that are presumed understood and remembered. Then the definitions must be memorized. An axiom is an assumption that starts a theory. It has to be memorized.

At the beginning of this book I mentioned the acronym FOIL, which is useful in solving algebraic equations; it stands for Firsts, Outers, Inners, Lasts. Look:

$$(a+b)(c+d)$$

You'd multiply the *firsts* (a and c), then the *outers* (a and d), then the inners (b and c), and then the *lasts* (b and d). Therefore, after applying FOIL, $(X+Y)(X+Y)$ would equal

$$X^2 \quad + \quad XY \quad + \quad YX \quad + \quad Y^2$$

$\uparrow$	$\uparrow$	$\uparrow$	$\uparrow$
Firsts	Outers	Inners	Lasts

Yes, acronyms do come in handy. One that's been around for a long time will help you remember the proper order for solving an equation. *The Princeton Review* mentions it in *Cracking the System*. The acronym is PEMDAS, and one way to remember it is to think of the sentence "Please Excuse My Dear Aunt Sally." It means Parentheses (clear them, which means to do the operations contained within them first); Exponents (take care of them); then Multiply, Divide, Add, and Subtract — *in that order*.

According to *Cracking the System*, two quadratic expressions appear over and over again on the SAT tests. It is suggested that you "train yourself to recognize them instantly" — in other words, *memorize* them.

$$X^2 - Y^2 = (X + Y)(X - Y)$$
$$X^2 + 2XY + Y^2 = (X + Y)^2$$

You might do it this way: Oxen (X^2) help a *miner* (minus); the miner emits a big **yawn** (Y^2); a *flag* (=) yawns; *eggs* (X) fall out of the flag, the eggs *applaud* (plus) a bottle of *wine* (Y), wine spills over *dimes* (times), dimes lay *eggs* on a *mynah* bird (minus), the mynah drinks a bottle of *wine* (Y). Include bowlegs at the proper places if you feel the need. See these pictures and review the Link and the equation. Then "do" the second one:

Oxen *applaud* because they need take **no** X-ray (2XY); you see an X-ray of a *cross* (+); it makes you **yawn** (Y^2); a *flag* yawns; you wave a flag as *eggs* (X) put *crosses* (+) on bottles of *wine* (Y); you say **no** (^{2}) — or the bottles are **new**. Form your own pictures.

I want to talk about algebraic and trigonometric laws, axioms, and theorems, but I'd like to stay with formulas and charts that include numbers for a while. In order to do that I'll have to jump around a bit. An equation for the law of cosines:

$$c^2 = a^2 + b^2 - 2ab \cos \angle C$$

Start with something that reminds of cosine (*cosign* or *cousin*). I'd then just visualize (as I cosign) a *can* on an *awn* applauding a *bean*.

If you need to be reminded of the equals sign, see the can waving a flag. Continue: the bean tries to *nab* a *miner* ($-2ab$) who *goes* (cos) at an angle ($\angle$) into the *sea* (C).

It's easy to memorize molecular compositions. I use words that remind of letters *and* numbers at the same time, as I've already taught. H_2SO_4 is sulfuric acid. It's quick and easy to learn if you see yourself pouring sulfuric acid on a hen, which makes the *hen sore*: **hen** for H_2, **sore** for SO_4. If you feel you need a reminder for "sulfuric," you can use *sell fur*.

The formula for glucose is $C_6H_{12}O_6$. This is one of the formulas I taught 40 years ago, and I receive calls to this day from people telling me they've never forgotten it. I said to visualize *Cash Hittin' Ouch!* Cash is C_6 and Hittin' is H_{12} and Ouch is O_6. *Glue coats* would remind you of glucose, so imagine someone is gluing coats, cash (bills or coins) is hittin' him, and he yells "Ouch!"

This leads to an equation involving starch:

$$nC_6H_{12}O_6 \longrightarrow (C_6H_{10}O_5)n + nH_2O$$

A *starched* shirt to **no** *cash hittin' ouch* to *arrow* to *cash hits owl* to *hen applauds* to *Noah* **nose**. The "s" sound in "nose" *will* remind you of the O (letter symbol for oxygen). However, if you prefer to use *owe*, or oxygen itself, do so — from *Noah*, associate to *hen* breathing lots of *oxygen*. You probably know that H_2O is water, so you could associate *hen applauds hen* to *water*. Always use any knowledge you already possess.

It doesn't matter how long or complicated equations are or seem. They would seem to be that way *whether or not* you apply my system! Here's the basic equation for photosynthesis:

$$6CO_2 + 6H_2O \xrightarrow[\text{chlorophyll}]{\text{light}} C_6H_{12}O_6 + 6O_2$$

You're taking a *photo* (photosynthesis) of a *shoe* that's a *con* ($6CO_2$), the con *applauds*, then you applaud lots of *ash* (6) falling into *water* (H_2O), the water *yields* (the arrow means "yields"; if you don't know that, use *arrow*) and turns *light green* (light, chlorophyll); light green *cash* is *hittin'* someone who yells "*Ouch*," but *applauds* as he starts **chasin'** ($6O_2$) you. (If you don't think the **s** sound in *chasin'* will remind you of the capital letter O, you can use *shone*; the "oh" sound is the O reminder.)

Would you like to try some short ones on your own? The chemistry textbooks I've checked all suggest that you learn (memorize) the names *and* formulas of the common acids. Remove the drudgery by applying the system. A list of some acids and their formulas follows. Use whatever comes to you first — either a word or phrase that includes letters and numbers, as I've done, or the letter words and phonetic words. One example, for the first item: *I see Dick* **hackin'** (HC_2) a **ham** (H_3) that you **own** (O_2). We've already done sulfuric acid, and you *can* use **handsome** for sulfurous (*sew for us*) because you'd *know* that the "d" isn't used; picturing a **hansom** cab is perfect.

acetic $HC_2H_3O_2$	nitrous HNO_2
boric H_3BO_3	oxalic $H_2C_2O_4$
carbonic H_2CO_3	perchloric $HClO_4$
hydrochloric HCl	phosphoric H_3PO_4
hydrocyanic HCN	sulfuric H_2SO_4
nitric HNO_3	sulfurous H_2SO_3

An association of the acid's name to its formula is all that's needed. Make the associations, then go over them, and you'll know the formulas for the common acids.

Cyclical structural formulas and straight-chain structural formulas are difficult to remember because you're working with shapes and similar symbols. Well, it's when the material is difficult that the memory systems reveal their true worth! Some standards should be incorporated. For example, you may want to use *bubble gum* or a *double* (as in baseball) or just *bond* to represent *double bond*. Single bonds are understood, but you can make up a standard word for that, too.

There are many C's, O's, H's, and N's in these formulas; you'll want clear, strong pictures to represent them. I use a beard (for *old*) to represent O (no, it won't conflict with *Noah*, your Peg Word for 2, because there are no numbers involved here). I use a birthday cake (which reminds me of *age*) for H. You can use *itch*, if you prefer. It's good to have a few words to represent each, so *hitch* and *ache* would also represent H, just as *open, hope,* and *eau* could also represent O. You can use *sea* or *see* for C, and *hen, end,* or *enemy* for N.

This is the cyclical structural formula for pyrimidine thymine:

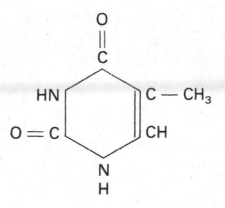

The first problem is the shape of the formula. No problem remembering it if you make it part of your Link. To do this, you might start with a Substitute Word for *thymine* associated to anything that reminds you of the shape. Or, you can use *shoe*, to remind you that it's a *six*-sided figure. Then, always start your Link from a definite point in that shape. I would always use either 11 or 12 o'clock, whichever is *there*; always start with 12 o'clock if there is a definite 12-o'clock point, as there is in this one, and always work clockwise.

Although I use *Noah* in this Link, I also use *beard*; if you think that would confuse you, you can use *wrinkles* to represent O (*old —* or *open*, and so on). So, you *tie* a *mine* (thymine) to keep a gigantic X from escaping. It escapes anyway, the X is *gone* (hexagon). The gigantic X has a long *beard* (O) and it hits a *double* into the *sea* (double bond, C).

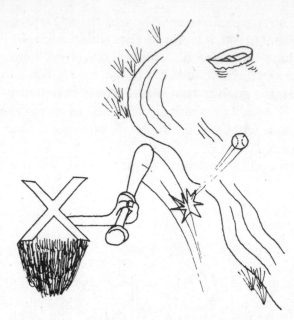

In the *sea*, the X's **chum** (C—CH_3) catches the ball; the chum chews *bubble gum* (double bond); a large bubble gum accepts **cash** (or sneezes, **ach**oo) to bring to **Noah** (or to Noah's ark); Noah *sees trouble* (C, double bond) ahead and puts on a beard (O) as a disguise; a *hen* (HN) falls out of the beard.

If you think "hen" would confuse because it's a letter word, use **hone** for HN. It really shouldn't matter. Don't overlook the essential points: Original Awareness (true memory) and the fact that you have some knowledge of the material. Those are the things that tell you that *hen* represents HN here, *not* N or H_2, even though I've used hen to represent that, too. Again, true memory and prior knowledge will tell you the difference. For NH, suppose you visualized a hen walking *backward* — that would work, if *you* thought of it.

I've used *double* and *bubble gum* and *trouble* to show you the different ways you can remind yourself of the same information (double bond, in this case). You can do that or use the same one each time. You can also use *sea* and *itch* for CH.

Okay, then; mentally review the Link (mine or yours), then draw the formula for pyrimidine (*pie rim dine*) thymine. I want you to see for yourself just how well the systems work! Then look at the straight chain structural formula for pyruvic acid:

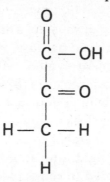

This would be a simple straight Link if it weren't necessary to know when to go off to the right and to the left to add elements. That's easily handled if you decide on a standard for *right* and a standard for *left*. I use a red flag (Communism) to remind me of *left* and a punch (right cross) for *right*. When you've decided on standards, a straight Link does the job. (For a straight-chain formula written left to right, you'd need standards for *up* and *down*.) You'd start with a word or phrase to remind you of pyruvic acid, then — *old* to *double* to *sea* to *right* to *"oh!"* to *see right trouble old*, and so forth.

I've touched on different kinds of formulas so that you know how to handle all kinds and so that you can see that the systems, with a bit of imagination, *can* handle any memory problem. To prove the point: the Lewis electron dot diagrams show the structure of atoms. Students have told me that they're impossible to memorize (not so!).

How would you go about memorizing these?

Be·   ·Ṅ: HE: ·Ḃ·   :F̈:   Li·   ·Ö: Ȧl   ·Ċ·

You'd have to know the symbol and how many dots go where. My solution, as usual, is to make symbol and dots meaningful. In order to do that, I've devised a simple pattern: **T** or **D** will always mean *one* dot (because **T** or **D** is your sound for 1), **N** will always mean *two* dots (**N** is the sound for 2), and **S** will mean *no* dots (**S** is the sound for zero).

Part of the pattern is always to start at the top and move clockwise. That's all you need because, now, one word or phrase associated with the element symbol will *tell* you the electronic symbol. For **Ḃe·** — you can see a *bee* (B) stinging an *eel* (e) at high tide. The **t** and **d** in "tide" tell you that a single dot goes on top and, since you're moving clockwise, a single dot goes to the right. (Had you associated the symbol to *test*, that would have meant one dot on top, none at right, one at bottom.) The element name is beryllium. If you wanted to remember that, you'd get *berry ill* into the picture.

A *bean totes tea*. That tells you that the symbol is B and that starting from the top and moving clockwise, the dot configuration is 1,1,0,1. So **·Ḃ·** is what you'd write, or remember. For **·N̈:** — associate *hen* with *tended* or *dented*. Do you see? That tells you that the dot pattern is 1,2,1,1.

For **HE:** — *he* to *sun* (or *sin*); **:F̈:** — *half* (or *effort* or *effervescent*) to *nun dine* (2,2,1,2); **Li·** — *lie* (or *el* train and *eye*) to *sit* (or *set* or *sewed*); **·Ö:** — *old* to *nun died* (or *knee noted*); **Aİ** — your friend Al to *tie* (or *tea*); **·Ċ·** — *sea* to *tied tight* (or *dotted*).

The electronic dot diagram is about as abstract an example as I could find.

I want you to realize that there is nothing too abstract to learn/memorize with my systems!

Chemistry, Biology, and Genetics

• • •

Tables, Laws, Theories, and Other Toughies

Letters, numbers, and names are the most difficult things to memorize ordinarily, and they're exactly what you *do* have to memorize in chemistry, biology, genetics, and similar subjects. I was recently shown a table of common ions and their charges (valences, really) by a high-school student who told me it would be a great help if he could memorize the entire thing. The table appears below. After you've looked at it, I'll show you the strategy I used to solve the memory problem. Then, if this is something you need to know, you'll be able to learn it in a short time. Even if you don't need to know it, I want you to see how it's "patternized."

+1	+2	+3
ammonium, NH_4^+	barium, Ba^{++}	aluminum, Al^{+++}
copper (1), Cu^+	calcium, Ca^{++}	chromium (111), Cr^{+++}
potassium, K^+	copper (11), Cu^{++}	iron (111), Fe^{+++}
silver, Ag^+	iron (11), Fe^{++}	
sodium, Na^+	lead (11), Pb^{++}	
	magnesium, Mg^{++}	
	nickel (11), Ni^{++}	
	zinc, Zn^{++}	

−1	−2	−3
acetate, $C_2H_3O_2^-$	carbonate, $CO_3^=$	phosphate, $PO_4^{\equiv}$
bromide, Br^-	chromate, $CrO_4^=$	
chlorate, ClO_3^-	oxide, $O^=$	
chloride, Cl^-	peroxide, $O_2^=$	
fluoride, F^-	sulfate, $SO_4^=$	
hydrogen carbonate, HCO_3^-	sulfide, $S^=$	
hydrogen sulfate, HSO_4^-	sulfite, $SO_3^=$	
hydroxide, OH^-		
iodide, I^-		
nitrate, NO_3^-		
nitrite, NO_2^-		

The charges (+1, +2, −1, and so on) are important to know. The strategy I use is similar to the one I use to create the Memory Graph. Make up a *heading* word that tells you whether it's plus or minus and plus or minus *how much*. Let **pl** mean "plus" and let the next consonant sound tell you whether it's plus 1, plus 2, or plus 3. **Plate, plot,** and **plod** are all good for +1. **Plane** or **plan**, within this pattern, can represent only +2, and **plum** must represent +3.

Let **mi** be "minus." Then, apply the same strategy: **mite, mitt** or **mighty** would tell you −1; **mine, mind,** or **mint** would tell you −2; and **mime** or **mimic,** −3. Select the word you like for each category and, suddenly, the digits and the plus and minus signs become *tangible* and can be pictured in your mind. Suddenly the problem is no longer insoluble.

You have choices to make; decide now whether to Link the ions by name, by symbol, or by both. Then decide whether you should start a Link with the plus or minus word then continue the Link with the ions, or whether you should associate *each* ion with its plus or minus word. Either way is all right. Example: You can start with *plane* (+2) and associate that to *bury him* (barium), or to **bar** or **bah** (Ba), or to *bean ape*. Then, associate whatever you've "used" for barium or Ba to calcium or Ca; Link that in turn to copper or Cu, and so on. The other way is to associate *barium* to *plane*, then make a separate association of *calcium* to *plane*, then *copper* to *plane*, *iron* to *plane*, and so on, all the way down the list until *zinc* to *plane*.

Now, the plus or minus sign after each ion symbol is unimportant because your plus or minus word tells you how many of which sign goes after each. The 1, 11, or 111 in parentheses after some items needn't be bothered with, but if you want to know which *do* have them, just put *bowlegs* into the pictures. As I said, even if this table isn't something you need for your studies, memorizing it lets you learn a "pattern" and get in some great practice.

At the beginning of most college biology textbooks, it is suggested that the student learn the terminology first so that he will know and understand what he reads and what his professor is talking about. Obviously.

It follows, then, that it would be much easier for you to study cells if you knew the parts of a typical animal-cell section. Suppose the parts you want to remember are Golgi body, centriole, nucleolus, nuclear membrane, cell membrane, mitochondrion, cytoplasm, and chromatin. Just Link your Substitute Words for the parts; start your Link with a picture of, perhaps, an *animal in a cell*.

Then — the animal has a *gold (gee!) body*, a gold body pushes a gigantic *cent* into a *roll*, a gigantic cent (or roll) uses a *new key* to release an *old ass*. The old ass has a *new clear brain*, the new clear brain is thrown into a *cell* with another *brain*, in that cell (with two brains now) is a *wet con dryin'* (perhaps wearing a *mitt*), or *mitt con dryin'* (mitochondrion); then the dryin' con starts to *sit* on a gigantic *toe* that's made of *plaster* (cytoplasm), the toe kicks some *chrome*, which dents easily because it's *tin* (*chrome tin* — chromatin). Do it, see the pictures — it takes very little time.

Exactly the same thing can be done to learn any list involving the structure of a cell (which is basic knowledge needed in the study of biology). Some of the parts listed below are the same as above, so you have a little help with the Substitute Words. Form your own Link (start with *cell struck chair*): cell membrane, cytoplasm, nucleus, nuclear membrane, endoplasmic reticulum, ribosomes, mitochondria, vacuoles.

*   *   *

You can use the letter words to help you visualize groups of letters like DNA, RNA, ADP, and so on, but there's another way to make such letter groups meaningful. (Whichever is used is then associated to the Substitute Words for the meanings.) DNA is deoxyribonucleic acid. A *dean* holding a *hen* in one hand and an *ape* in the other reminds you of DNA, but so does a girl named **Dinah**. Dinah puts a large *D* on an *ox*, tying it on with a *ribbon* that's *new* and makes a *click*. RNA is ribonucleic acid; if you know DNA, just drop the "deoxy" or associate your letter words for RNA to *ribbon nuclear* (or use **arena** for RNA).

ADP is adenosine diphosphate. **Add** up (or **a d**ope) or an *ape* and a *dean* eating a *pea* would remind you of ADP. You might picture yourself *add*ing up all the *sign*s in a *den*, and perhaps the signs are shaped like *O*'s (*add den O sign*); a diver comes to help and drowns — a *diver's fate* (diphosphate).

Knowing ADP aids in knowing ATP, which is adenosine triphosphate (just get the "tri" in there). But you can make a completely separate association. A *teepee* is adding signs in a den, and so on, to *driver's fate*.

IAA is indole acetic acid. A gigantic *eye* saying "*aye aye*" or an *eye* and two *apes* will remind you of IAA. Connect either one to *in the hole* and *a seat* (and *acid*, if you feel it necessary). NAA is naphthalene acetic acid. See yourself neighing (*neigh*: NAA) as you *nap* while *lean*ing and *see* your friend *Dick* (*nap-lean-I-see-Dick*). You can get *tall* in there for *nap tall lean*. Always your choice.

DPN is diphosphopyridine nucleotide. The letter words or *dippin'* would work. Perhaps, you *die fast* because a *foe* comes *piratin'* out of the water, but you're *dippin'* into a *new, clear tide* first.

Would you like to prove the effectiveness of the technique to yourself? Good. Go over the example associations, or form your own, then fill in these blanks:

DNA is _____

RNA is _____

ADP is _____

ATP is _____

IAA is _____

NAA is _____

DPN is _____

I've yet to find an academic memory problem that can't be solved by applying one of the ideas I've already discussed. Biology students who want to remember the elements found in protoplasm think of the phrase "C. Hopkins Café, Mg." This memory aid works if the student knows the elements and just needs the reminder of the first letters or symbols. The letters in the phrase stand for carbon, hydrogen, oxygen, phosphorus, K (the *symbol* for potassium), iodine, nitrogen, sulfur, Ca (the symbol for calcium), Fe (the symbol for iron), and Mg (the symbol for magnesium). To help remember the acronym itself, you might think of "See (C) Hopkins Café? Mighty good!"

A fairly typical question on college biology exams is "Trace the path of a molecule of blood from the heart to the thumb(nail)." If you form a Link of the necessary Substitute Words when you originally read or hear the information, you'll know the answer immediately. You might start the Link with a *mole* that's *cool* and *bleeding* (your heading picture). Associate that to *"a order art airy"* (aorta artery). Or, just see the cool mole forcing itself out of the heart via the largest artery, the aorta.

Link whatever you're using to, perhaps, *brake EO see fall lick trunk* (brachiocephalic trunk). A *sub* made of *clay* (subclavian artery) comes out of the trunk; an *ax* that's *ill* (axillary artery) wrecks the sub; the ax *breaks* and becomes more *ill* (brachial artery). The broken pieces of the ax turn into *radios* (or use *ray dial* — radial artery). The radios have *dorsal* fins and swim on a *pole* with some *asses* (dorsalis pollicis artery).

* * *

For chemistry, it would help to remember the kinetic-molecular theory of gases, which assumes that:

1. A gas is composed of tiny, individual particles. (See a gigantic *tie* [1] breaking up into tiny, individual particles.)
2. Particles of a gas are separate from each other and are in continuous, random motion. They travel in straight-line paths until a collision deflects them onto new straight-line paths. (The hairs of a beard [*Noah*, 2] separate and fly off in random directions. See them traveling straight until they hit one another and go off in other straight lines.)
3. When a collision occurs between two particles, energy may be transferred from one to the other, but no energy is lost or converted into heat. (Your *ma* [3] collides with another ma; both lose no energy nor do they get warmer; see them transferring things to each other.)
4. Particles of a gas do not interact with one another; they have no attraction for one another. (Bottles of *rye* [4] ignore one another and have absolutely no attraction for one another.)
5. The volume of the particles is so small compared to the total volume of the gas that it is negligible. The volume of gas is composed mostly of empty space. (Visualize so few policemen [*law*, 5] in the vast scheme of things that they're negligible. They float around in empty space.)

I've used the first five Peg Words for this because the items were numbered when the information was shown to me. I also think that memorizing them by number is a bit more *definite* than Linking them. But that may not be so for you. Sure you can Link them. Start with a "heading" Substitute Word or phrase for "kinetic-molecular"; *can attic mole cool*, perhaps. If you learn it as I've suggested, with the Peg Words, you can still include *can attic*, and so on, in each picture, if you like. I don't find it necessary.

Bear in mind that I am not studying the subjects discussed here, nor those in the next chapter, and I don't know as much about them as you might. I may use reminders where you don't need to use them, and you may be able to visualize the thing itself — no

Substitute Word needed. The application of the techniques is an individual thing; each person will handle it a bit differently, which is as it should be. What's important is that they *work*.

What you're learning here and in the next chapter is basically how to remember *what you read*. That's very important; I'll devote a separate chapter to it shortly.

Chapter 22

More Toughies Tamed

• • •

Physics, Astronomy, Earth Science, Trigonometry, Geometry, and Chemistry

*I*n this chapter I want to show you how to handle various kinds of information in several subjects, some of which I've already discussed. It's good practice for you, and it will continue to lead you toward the goal of being able to learn as you read.

Basic Scientific Principles

Try to memorize these basic concepts of science:

1. Energy can be changed into other forms of energy. Matter can be changed into other forms of matter. Matter can be changed into energy. However, the total amount of matter and energy remains the same.
2. The universe is in constant change.
3. Living things exchange matter and energy with their environment.
4. All organisms are the product of their heredity and environment acting together.
5. Organisms are in constant change.

You should have memorized these easily by number, using your Peg Words or a simple Link. Some rapid-fire suggestions:

See a gigantic letter G on your *tie*; something *enters* the G (*enter G* — energy; or use a chocolate bar to represent energy) and changes the *form* of the G (energy can be changed into other forms of energy). The G (or the tie) gets *madder* and madder (matter), and then it gets mad in a *different* way (matter can be changed into other forms of matter).

Someone gets *madder* and madder as he tries to *enter* a G (matter can be changed to energy). He tries, but the G doesn't budge (it remains the same) and he remains just as mad (the total amount of matter and energy remains the same).

For teaching purposes, I've put every fact into the association. You probably wouldn't do that; if you understand the concept in the first place, something to remind you of *energy* and *matter* is probably all you'd need. And I'm breaking down each word for you. I would use *gravy tea* as an example of a substitute phrase for *gravity* when teaching, although if I were memorizing the information, I'd just see something *falling*. I want you to understand this: you can use whatever fleeting picture runs through your mind when you think of any particular concept. My examples must be understood by all; what you use has to make sense only to you. This holds true for all my examples.

All right, let's complete this example.

See *Noah* (2) holding the universe on his head as he *constantly changes* positions.

Your *ma* (3) is *entering* a G and getting *madder* as she *exchanges living things* for a *hen, wire,* and *mint* (environment).

A *rye* (4) bread is playing the *organ* as a *hare ready*ing *tea* (heredity) and a *hen* wrapped in *wire* and sucking a *mint* (environment) *act together*.

An *organ* is being arrested by a policeman (*law,* 5); it *constantly changes* size and shape.

These are the first pictures that came to my mind to remember these concepts by number. It might be better and faster for you to Link them. All you really need is one *key* word or thought for each concept.

Now let's turn to specific subject areas.

Physics

Similar to the last example in the preceding chapter (the kinetic-molecular theory) is the information needed in order to answer this question from a college physics exam: "What are Kepler's three laws?" They're handled basically the same way. First, the laws:

1. Every planet moves about the sun in an elliptical orbit having the sun at one focus.
2. If a line is drawn from the sun to a planet, it will pass over equal areas in equal intervals of time.
3. The cube of the average orbital radius R, divided by the square of its period T, is a constant.

I'll tell you how I memorized them; do it my way or your own. I did it by number, using the Peg Words. If you want to, use a Substitute Word or phrase for "Kepler" in each association (*cap low* or *kerplunk*). See *ties* (1) moving about the sun in elliptical orbits; the sun is always within.

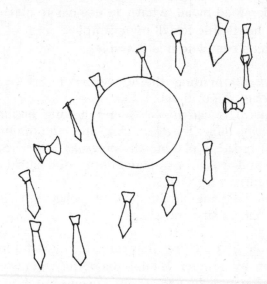

You can put *oar bits* in there, if you like. If you see *caps low* beneath the ties, you have the Kepler reminder.

A man with a long beard (*Noah*, 2) is drawing a line from the sun to a planet (or *plan it*). See him doing this (from sun to planet) with other planets at the *same time* (equal), or visualize him drawing the lines with an *American flag* (equal). You can also see him throwing a *pass* over *equal areas*. Use what you feel will remind you of what you want to be reminded of.

A *cube* is really an *average radio* (radius) with a large *R* on it, and it's in *orbit*. It's hit and broken up (*divided*) by a *square* cup of *tea* (T) that has many dots (*period*) in it. This happens *constantly*. Your *ma* (3) drinks all the tea.

Astronomy

Mentioning the planets reminds me to remind you that it's easy to form a Link of Substitute Words and phrases to help you remember the planets in order — that is, according to their distance from the sun: Mercury (closest to sun), Venus, Earth, Mars, Jupiter, Saturn, Uranus, Neptune, and, finally, Pluto.

If you already know the planet names and need reminders only, you can do it by thinking of this silly phrase: "**Move my J** (at) **sunup**." Or, get this sentence in mind: "**My vicious enemy made a judge serve us new punishment**." The extra "a" can be used to remind you of the asteroids (minor planets).

Still, the best way to remember the planets is to Link your Substitute Words, since you want to remember a sequence. Here are some suggestions for the words or phrases or pictures you might want to use:

> *Mercury* — thermometer, murky, me cure E, my curry, Madame Curie
> *Venus* — V nuts, vein, Goddess of Love, V nose
> *Earth* — dirt, (your own) home
> *Mars* — mars (damages), ma's, Mars bar
> *Jupiter* — shoe pitter, you be there, juniper berries
> *Saturn* — sat (on) urn, sad turn
> *Uranus* — you rain (on) us, rain nose, you're on us
> *Neptune* — nab tune, nip tune, God of the Sea
> *Pluto* — blue toe, blew toe, Pluto (the dog)

You could, of course, remember them by number: associate the Substitute Word to the correct Peg Word (1 to 9) — or rhyme word (*gun* to *vine*) — and you've got it!

Earth Science

A typical item on a high-school science test is "Name the five main gases found in our atmosphere." The answer: nitrogen, oxygen, argon, carbon dioxide, water vapor. Link *night row (gem), ox itch, R gone, carbon die ox hide, water pour* (or water turning into steam — vapor).

The layers of the atmosphere are troposphere, stratosphere, mesosphere, thermosphere, and ionosphere. To remember them, Link *throw pole* to *straight O* to *mess o'* to *thermos* to *eye on* (or *iron*).

Trigonometry and Geometry

The law of sines says: **In a triangle, the ratio of any side to the sine of the opposite angle is constant.** You can start the Link with a picture of *signs* serving as members of a *jury*. See that jury (law) of signs sitting in a large *triangle* instead of a jury box; there's a gigantic *radio* (ratio) on a *side* of the triangle; *opposite* the radio is a sign with a *halo* or a *bent metal rod* (halo for "angel" or the bent rod for "angle" — either will remind you of angle); the halo or angle never moves, it remains *constant*.

I've already discussed how to remember the law of cosines in equation form, but you also might want to learn it in verbal form: **In a triangle, the square of any side is equal to the sum of the squares of the other two sides minus twice the product of those sides and the cosine of the angle included between them.** A *policeman* (law) is *cosign*ing a contract on a *triangular* piece of paper. That paper flies into a *boxing ring* (square) and fights at *any side*; it waves an *American flag* (is equal to) as it fights; *some other boxing rings* (sum of the squares) come from *other sides* (of the other sides); a *miner* brings up his *product twice* (minus twice the product) and places some of it on the *sides* of these other boxing rings, then *cosigns*, with a *bent piece of iron* the contract lying *between them* (and the cosine of the angle included between them).

Consider the following theorems and the ways I would memorize (learn) them.

The sine, cosine, secant, and cosecant functions have the period 2π. The tangent and cotangent functions have the period π. A large *sign* (sine) is *cosign*ing (cosine) a contract; it takes a *second* (secant) for it to *function*, then a *coat* runs over for a *second* (cosecant), makes a *period* and gets *two pies* (2π) in the face; a *tan gent* (tangent) wearing a *coat* (cotangent) attends a function where he is served *one pie, period* (period π).

You'll soon start using the same Substitute Words to represent the same concepts; they become standards, like *boxing ring* for "square," *cosign* for "cosine," *bent metal rod* for "angle." I always visualize half a grapefruit to remind me of *half*.

If two parallel lines are cut by a transversal, each pair of corresponding angles is congruent. A *train reverses* (transversal) and *cuts both railroad tracks* (two parallel lines); this separates the *two* (a pair) *bent metal rods* (angles — or use *angels*) who *correspond* with a *con* who *grew* a gigantic *ant* (corresponding angles are congruent).

In a plane, if a line is perpendicular to one of two parallel lines, it is perpendicular to the other. In an *airplane*, a *clothesline* is *upright* (perpendicular) on *one* of a *pair of railroad tracks* (two parallel lines). Now see it jumping *perpendicularly* onto the *other* track.

Through a given point, there passes one and only one line perpendicular to a given plane. Someone *gives* you a *point*; one *clothesline*, and *only one*, is *upright* (perpendicular — or you can use *per pen*) and *passes* through this point to *give* you an *airplane*.

Two lines perpendicular to the same plane are coplanar. *Two clotheslines* (or *lions*) are *upright* on the *same airplane*; they're planning something together — they're *coplanners*.

If two triangles have the same altitude h, then the ratio of their areas is equal to the ratio of their bases. *Two triangles* are flying at the *same altitude*; each has an *itch* (h); a *radio* (ratio) is playing an *aria* (area) for the triangles and waving an *American* *flag* (equal) as a *race* between an *E* and an *O* (*race E O* — ratio) goes around the *bases*.

If one leg of a right triangle is half as long as the hypotenuse, then the opposite angle measures 30. A *triangle* is throwing a punch (*right* cross); it has two *legs*, *one* of which is *half as long* as the other. See a *high pot in use* (perhaps as a perch for the short leg). A *bent metal rod* (angle) is sitting *opposite* the high pot (opposite angle) on a *mouse* (30), *measuring* it.

Chemistry

Concepts in chemistry like the following often must be memorized.

1. When an atom is not neutral, it is an ion.
2. An ionic bond is formed when two atoms are drawn to each other by opposite charges.
3. A covalent bond is formed when electrons are shared.
4. Molecules can be formed only by covalent bonding.
5. Organic molecules contain carbon.
6. Molecules always vibrate.

You could use your basic Peg Words or the rhyming words (*gun* to *sticks*) to learn these basics, although I don't think you need any number reminders in this case. Form your *own* ridiculous pictures to remind you of what you want to remember; do it on your own and you'll find the material is virtually memorized by that effort alone! My helping you is not really helping you; you're better off imagining your own pictures, as I've already told you. But here's how I'd do it:

1. An *atom* (*Adam*, or *atom bomb*) is *not* getting a *new trial* (not neutral); it's made of *iron* (or its name is *Ian* — ion).
2. *Two atom bombs* are being *drawn* (with pen and ink) *together*. I'm *opposed* to this so I *charge* them (opposite charges), and I also *nick* the *bond* (ionic bond) between them.
3. *Electric trains* (electrons) are being *shared* by children sleeping under a *coverlet* (covalent), which is a large savings *bond*.

4. A *coverlet* that is really a large *bond* is forming *cool moles* (or *Molly cools* — molecules).
5. *Cool moles* are playing the *organ* (organic) on a giant sheet of *carbon* paper.
6. *Moles* are so *cool* that they *shiver* (vibrate) *continually*.

It's important for you to understand that in this example and those that follow (as in those that came before), I'm using Substitute Words where you may not need them. I've said this before, but it warrants repetition. You may want reminders where I didn't bother with them because I didn't think I needed them. *You* have to make those choices.

Chapter 23

Reading and Listening
. . .
No Note-taking Necessary!

*M*uch of the information we learn in school and elsewhere is ingested through *reading*. Everything I've taught you up to now applies to remembering *as you read*. The first thing to do is to read the material once, quickly, to make sure it's something you really want to learn. (Reading is usually a search for information, a search for answers.) Then, read it again, applying the systems to remind you of important facts. Read this excerpt once.

GREECE

Across the Mediterranean Sea from Egypt is a rocky peninsula with an uneven coastline. This is the mainland of Greece. East of that peninsula, in the Aegean Sea, are lots of islands, some large and some small. These lands were the home of Greek civilization.

The first Greeks probably came to the region about 2000 BC. By 1500 BC, some of them had formed a civilization. They learned how to write and paint, and they built great palaces. But they spent most of their time fighting. About 1100 BC, they were conquered by other Greek tribes who were less civilized.

Start with a Substitute Word for the heading "Greece." In some cases, forming a Link of just the headings of a chapter or a book will remind you of the vital information in that chapter or book. Don't overlook this idea. You can go through a book once or twice and know all the main points in sequence by Linking the chapter headings, or the bold type. In this example, we'll Link the important facts *to* the heading. Work with me now, because I'll test you later just so that you can see what you've accomplished.

For the heading, *grease*. There is lots of grease on a *cross*; the cross dives into the *sea* to *meditate* (across the Mediterranean Sea); then that cross swims from a *pyramid* (or Sphinx — Egypt) to a gigantic *pen* (taking *insulin*, perhaps — peninsula) that's writing *unevenly* on a *rock*; the rock *coasts* over the *mane* of a *greasy* lion and *lands*.

Review: You've reminded yourself that across the Mediterranean Sea from Egypt is a rocky peninsula with an uneven coastline — the mainland of Greece.

Imagine lots of *yeast* (or *eats*) landing. The yeast grows a gigantic beard that looks like a gigantic *pen* — it's *aging* (east of the *pen*insula, in the Aegean Sea). The beard (pen) breaks up into *lots of large and small* pieces that form *islands*. Pieces of *grease* start to live together *civilly*, building *homes* (home of Greek civilization).

A gigantic *nose* is built. (*Nose* is your basic Peg Word for 20. You'd know that this is a reminder for **2000** BC. If you don't think so, you can use **noises** sue or **nice** sis. You can also use **Bic** [pen] to remind you of BC — which is really not necessary, because you'd *know* it isn't AD 2000!)

A gigantic *towel* (15 — **1500** BC) is covering the homes and the nose. See people *writing* and *painting* on the towel. One of the paintings is of a *great palace*; the writers and painters *fight* over this painting *most of the time*. An *uncivilized tot* (11 — **1100** BC) *conquers* the people who are fighting.

I've included *all* the facts. Usually, one key picture will remind you of a *few* facts. Always include what *you* need to be reminded of. Review the Link, then fill in these blanks:

Across the _____ sea from _____ is a rocky _____ with an _____ coastline. This is the _____ of Greece. East of that _____, in the _____ Sea, are lots of _____, some _____ and some _____. These lands were the home of Greek _____.

The first Greeks probably came to the region about _____ BC. By _____ BC, some of them had formed a _____. They learned how to _____ and _____, and they built great _____. But they spent most of their time _____. About _____ BC, they were _____ by other Greek tribes who were less _____.

If you made a good Link (really "saw" the pictures), you breezed through this test. If you didn't, go over the Link and then try these:

In about what year did some Greeks have a civilization? _____ BC

Describe the shape of the coastline of Greece in one word. _____

What country is across the Mediterranean Sea from Greece? _____

The first Greeks probably arrived in the area about _____ BC.

The Greek islands are in the _____ Sea.

What happened about 1100 BC? _____

The Aegean Sea is _____ (*north, west, east, or south?*) of the peninsula.

In addition to writing, painting, and building palaces, the Greeks spent most of their time doing what? _____

I purposely mixed up the questions in order to show you that you would still pass the test easily. That's important; you knew the answers to questions asked in any order, even though you memorized the information in sequence. Because, you see, once you know the information, you know it in *any* order.

You can memorize a poem — even if the lines don't rhyme (rhymes are a memory aid).

> *The sun peeks out*
> *   with one purple eye.*
> *Without a blink*
> *   it searches the world,*
> *   noiselessly sighing*
> *   it sleeps again.*

Start the Link with a picture of the sun peeking over the horizon with one gigantic eye (the sun peeks out). If you want a reminder of "purple," use a Substitute Word for it, perhaps a (purple) grape. The eye doesn't blink at all (without a blink). The sun holds a searchlight and searches all over (it searches the world). The searchlight sighs heavily (or it's a large *size* and *heavy*) without a sound (noiselessly sighing), and lies down to sleep (it sleeps again). Go over this once or twice, and you'll *know* the poem (which I wrote just for this example).

To learn lines word for word, do the same thing; be a bit more specific perhaps, and go over it a few more times. From Shakespeare's *As You Like It*:

> *. . . the whining school-boy, with his satchel*
> *And shining morning face, creeping like a snail*
> *Unwillingly to school.*

A *schoolboy* is *whining* (or he's drinking *wine*); see him carrying *his satchel* (or a *sad shell*), or drinking wine from a satchel. There's a *face* on the satchel that is *shining* so brightly it turns night into *morning*. Now something is *creeping like a snail* and shining brightly. A gigantic snail is being dragged *unwillingly to school*.

The only way you can prove to yourself how quickly and well you can learn (memorize) poetry this way is by *doing* it. In most cases, it's necessary to remember only the main thoughts, then the incidentals — the ifs, ands, and buts — fall into place automatically. The English language itself is a memory aid.

The silly pictures won't keep running through your mind (if they did, it wouldn't hurt you any). Use the information a few times and it becomes knowledge; the silly pictures fade.

I mentioned "headings" earlier. You can create your own "headings" by highlighting the facts you feel are important for you to remember (learn). Effective reading is far more than just recognizing words. Passive reading must be changed to active, aggressive reading. For study purposes, that would entail the boiling down of hundreds of words to a few vital thoughts or facts. Effective reading is a search for ideas, thoughts, and answers.

Applying these memory techniques *forces* you to read effectively because you're forced to locate the vital, key thoughts. The search itself is a memory aid because you must concentrate as you do it. Then, lock in — *memorize* — the facts you locate as you locate them. Link them! Or highlight them first, then go back and Link them.

Keep at it, and before you know it you'll be memorizing reading material *as you read*. You may be forced to read more slowly than you usually do, but don't let that bother you. You'll be saving lots of time because you won't have to read the material over and over again! And you'll retain the information for as long as *you* want.

Besides reading, much of the information you remember/learn comes from *listening*. Applying the systems you've just learned is the best way to *focus* your attention and concentration as well as maintain that attention and concentration. The reason most people have trouble concentrating while listening is that they usually think four times faster than the speaker speaks; there's too much time available for the mind to wander.

The way to fill that time gap and to stop your mind from wandering is to apply the memory systems as the speaker or lecturer speaks. Then, there's neither time nor opportunity for mind wandering or daydreaming.

Listen closely for key words or thoughts; just as you'd search for them while reading, make up Substitute Words and Link them. Then, just as with reading, you've turned passive listening into active, effective listening/learning. If you take notes, all you really need to do is list the key words or thoughts. Then, Link them after the lecture.

What's important here is that listening for main points, which you *have to do* in order to apply the systems, is like grabbing your mind by the scruff of the neck and telling it, "Darn it, concentrate!" You're forcing it to be Originally Aware. Even if the association/ Linking doesn't work, you'll still remember more of any lecture than you ever have before. After some practice, which means *doing* it, you'll do it faster and faster, and have to take fewer and fewer written notes. Try it; what in the world do you have to lose?

Chapter 24

Literature and Art

. . .

*Why, Oh Why, Don't They
Teach This in School?*

$\mathcal{T}$he memory systems make the remembering of book and author, composition and composer, and painting and artist just about instantaneous. These are good examples of the entity-of-two aspect of memory problems. Usually, you want to learn more than just those two entities; you need to know the characters, plot, or theme of a novel, the "school" of an artist, and so forth.

Literature

I'll use *A Tale of Two Cities* by Charles Dickens as an example. The main characters in the novel are Charles Darnay, Sidney Carton, Madame Defarge, Lucie Manette, and Dr. Manette. The plot centers on the French Revolution and Carton's sacrifice (he dies in Darnay's place).

A gigantic *tail* has *two cities* on it; they *quarrel* (Charles) "like the *dickens*." One quarreler *darns* an *A* (Charles Darnay) *sitting* on a *carton* (Sidney Carton); an elegant lady (Madame) eats *the fudge* (Defarge) that's in the carton; it's awfully *loose* (Lucie) fudge and a *man ate* (or *my net* — Manette) it all; the man who ate puts on a *stethoscope* (Dr. Manette). For the plot, if it's necessary, you can visualize fighters or quarrelers speaking *French* (as they *revolve*, if you like — for French Revolution); a *carton dies* as the man *darning* an *A* walks away. Or, a *carton* hitting a *sacrifice* bunt (in baseball) so that the man *darn*ing an *A* on first base can get to second would remind you of that part of the plot.

Lillian Hellman wrote *Watch on the Rhine*. The primary characters are Kurt Mueller and Tek, and it is a play about a German refugee and a Nazi sympathizer meeting in an American home; the dominant motif is good versus evil. You have to decide what to include in your association; include only what you need as reminders.

You might try this association: See a *rhino* wearing a gigantic *watch* (*Watch on the Rhine*); a *lily*, covered with *Hellmann's* mayonnaise (Lillian Hellman), comes out of the watch. A *mule* (Mueller) hears the loud *tick* (Tek) of the watch; he's *curt* (Kurt) to the rhino. Perhaps the mule is wearing a *swastika* and the rhino *runs* toward an *American flag*, but the mule is there (that's the plot reminder — the German refugee and the Nazi meet in an American home). You could see the rhino being very *good* and the mule being *evil*. Do you see how valuable this idea is for exams and tests pertaining to literature?

Here are a few more examples of easy associations:

Rabbit, Run, by John Updike: See a *rabbit run*ning *up* a *dike*. (Sure, you can get a *john* into the picture if you think you'd need it.)

The Magic Barrel, by Bernard Malamud. A *barrel* does *magic* tricks.

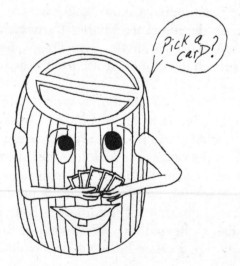

Then, you *mail mud* to it to stop it from *burn*ing *hard*.

Ulysses, by James Joyce. *You list E's* as someone *aims juice* (or *joys*) at you.

The Catcher in the Rye, by J. D. Salinger. A baseball *catcher* catches *rye* whiskey while *sailin'* a *jaw* (or *sail injure*) toward *jail* (J) where he meets a college *dean* (D).

Lord of the Flies, by William Golding. A gigantic fly *lord*s it over all the other *flies*; he writes his *will* on a *yam* with *gold ink*.

Invisible Man, by Ralph Ellison. A *rough* (Ralph — if you think you need a reminder for the first name) letter L (or *el* train) *is* your *son* (Ellison), and he fades into *invisibility*.

The Waste Land, by T. S. Eliot. A gigantic cup of *tea* (T) drives an *ess curve* (S) around a huge *lot* (or picture L E yacht) that's a *wasteland*.

Art

I discussed music appreciation — specifically, compositions and composers — in chapter 18. Exactly the same techniques can be applied to art appreciation.

Mondrian was a constructivist. See a *man dryin'* a huge *construction* site. If you see him dancing the boogie-woogie on Broadway, you'll also remember that Mondrian painted "Broadway Boogie-Woogie."

See a *doll* that's *sure real* to help you know that Dalí was a surrealist. See that doll on a flying horse (Pegasus, or *peg asses*) to remember that Dalí painted "Pegasus in Flight."

You *ran wire* to *impress* people tells you that Renoir was an impressionist. *Money* (Monet) *impresses* people — Monet was an impressionist.

Botticelli painted "The Birth of Venus." A *bottle* and a *cello* get together and manage to give *birth* to a *lady without arms* (or picture V's and *nuts*). Botticelli painted "The Calumny of Apelles"; associate *bottle cello* (or *bought jelly*) to *column knee* and *apples*.

Rauschenberg is known as a pop artist. See a *roach* on an iceberg drinking *pop*.

Edvard Munch (pronounced *Muhnk*) was an expressionist. You're trying to *express* yourself to a *monk*. Imagine the monk emitting a terrible scream (Munch painted "The Scream," one of my favorite paintings).

A *ram brand*ing a *human* reminds that Rembrandt was a humanist. See it done at *night* as people *watch* — Rembrandt painted "Night Watch."

So you see, you may not be interested in literature and art (although you should be, if you're studying them), but you sure can make it *seem* as if you're interested by knowing more about them than anyone else!

Chapter 25

Professional
Graduate School
• • •
Medicine and Dentistry —
Fewer Late Nights Cramming

*I*n chapter 2, I mentioned a couplet that reminds medical students of the first letters of the cranial nerves in anatomical order. But knowing the first letters doesn't always help. A Link of Substitute Words *does*. Start the Link with, perhaps, a *crane* with lots of *nerve*. See that crane working in an *old factory* (olfactory). Then "olfactory" to "optic": the entire *old factory* starts to *tick* loudly as it floats *up* (*up tick* — optic).

The loud tick, up high, is stopped by *a cool motor* (oculomotor). See a cool motor being *thrown clear* (trochlear). You throw a clear *gem*; *Al* tries it *on* (*try gem on Al* — trigeminal). You try on a gem but you only *have two cents* (abducens). You have only two cents, but it's enough to have a *facial* (facial nerve). You're having a facial in an *auditorium* (auditory). An auditorium is a *jail* for a *glossy pharaoh* (*glossy pharaoh in jail* — glossopharyngeal). The glossy jailed pharaoh goes to Las *Vegas* (or is *vague* — vagus). In Vegas, an *accessory* (accessory nerve) joins you, to help you gamble. The accessory waves to (or an *ax says sorry* to) a gigantic *hypodermic needle* that's *glossy* (hypoglossal).

Form the Link, see the pictures clearly, and you'll know the cranial nerves both in and out of order. A separate association will tell you the meaning of a word. An *old factory smelling bad* tells you that olfactory means "pertaining to smell."

Perhaps your assignment is to look at a diagram of the human skeleton and learn some of the major bones. Consider:

head — frontal, malar, maxilla, mandible
shoulder — clavicle
spinal column — cervical vertebrae, lumbar vertebrae
chest — sternum
pelvis — sacrum
arm — humerus, ulna, radius
hand — carpus, phalanges
leg — femur, patella, tibia, fibula
foot — tarsus, phalanges

The "heading" picture is a *skeleton*, of course. It is facing *front* and is very *tall* (frontal); a person keeps mailing letters from the front into a tall mailbox; he's a *mailer* (malar); a *Mack* truck mails letters and gets *ill* (*Mack's ill* — or *Max ill* — maxilla). An ill person has to *man the bull* (mandible) in the bullring. I've used reminders for the bones only; you can put in a word to remind you of location, although I don't think it's necessary.

Continue: A bull begins to *claw* a *vehicle* (clavicle); a vehicle *serves a cold* meal, and *brays* (*serve a cold bray* — cervical vertebrae). You probably wouldn't need the reminder for vertebrae. A cold meal is eaten by *lumber* (lumbar vertebrae) and the lumber eats *ham* that's *stern* (*stern ham* — sternum; or maybe *stir nun*); a stern ham carries a *sack* of *rum* (sacrum; the rum can be singing and moving like Elvis, if necessary, for *pelvis*); people laugh at this because it's *humorous* (humerus).

Laughing people scream "*Oh no*" (ulna — or, *owner* or *ol' knee*); millions of *radios* (radius) scream, "Oh no," as many carpets (carpus) fly out of the radios; a girl named *Fay lounges* (phalanges — or, *fail in juice*); she pays *more* of a *fee* to continue lounging (*fee more* — femur); you pay more of a fee to *pat Ella* (patella — or, *pa teller* or *pat teller*); Ella tips over more than anyone — she's *tippier* (tibia — or *tip ya*); a person who's tippier *fibs* about the *law* to you (*fib you law* — fibula); the person who fibs throws *tar* at you and your friends (*tars us* — tarsus); there's tar all over your *toes* (phalanges — or use *Fay lounges* again). Go over this once or twice and you won't have to "bone up" on these ever again.

Some parts of the human brain: cerebrum, cerebellum, medulla oblongata, pons, and diencephalon. If you're familiar with them and need only simple reminders, a Link of *broom* to *bell* to *dull* (or *dollar*) to *puns* to *dime save alone* would do it. Perhaps the sentence "Carrying cargo makes pants dirty" is all you need. Substitute Words make it more specific: *Sarah broom* for cerebrum, *dyin'* (to) *surf alone* or *Diane's F alone* for diencephalon, and so forth. You'd start your Link with "brain."

A dental student told me that he learned the names of the amino acids easily and quickly by Linking Substitute Words. Here's the list: alanine, glycine, valine, leucine, isoleucine, proline, phenylalanine, tyrosine, serine, threonine, methionine, arginine, histidine, lysine, aspartic acid, glutamic acid, hydroxyproline, hydroxylysine.

He knew which ones ended in "-ine" or "-nine," so no need to use the endings. Here's how he did it (the words in parentheses are what I might have used): *Alan* to *gloss* (glassy; listen) to *valet* (valley) to *loose* to *I sew loose* (ice so loose) to *pro* (prowlin') to *fan an E* singing *la la* (Fanny la la) to *Taurus* (tyros) to *sir* (serene) to *three O's* to *method* (met E O) to *aw gee* (Argentina; archin') to *history* (his tie dine) to *lies* to *a spare tick* to *glue atomic* to *hide rocks see pro* (hide rocks zebra) to *hide rocks see lie* (hide rock sea lies).

Those silly pictures come quite easily now. And if you're thinking that this is too much work — *don't*. It's much less work than using rote memory. Applying the techniques is the *easy* way; it's a challenge, it's fun, and it forces you to concentrate on the new material.

Chapter 26

The "Tablecloth" Chapter

• • •

Lots of Goodies

*F*riends tell me I have a "completion complex." I feel I have to complete each and every project I start and — call it a "tablecloth" complex — I have to *cover* every part, every corner, every aspect of that project (just as a tablecloth covers the entire top of the table). Well, that's not possible here, as I've already told you. But I'll use this chapter as my "tablecloth," to try to cover just a few more areas with short, quick examples.

U.S. Geography

See a gigantic *cow* covering the entire northwestern part of the United States to remind you that three northwestern states are California, Oregon and Washington. Think of "**UCAN** (you can) be in four states at once" and that will remind you of the only four states that all meet at a single point: Utah, Colorado, Arizona, and New Mexico.

Music

You're about to *stab* four singers (a quartet); that tells you that a quartet consists of a soprano, tenor, alto, and bass.

Social Studies

In a textbook on basic social studies, there's a list of explorers dating back to 2750 BC — Hannu of Egypt explored the land of Punt — all the way to Neil Armstrong "exploring" the moon in 1969. I've already used the example of the first man on the moon. For the first listing: you're holding a bunch of **nickels** (2750) in your *hand*; one nickel becomes a giant letter *U* (*hand U* — Hannu). The U (or *ewe*) climbs a *pyramid* (or a *sphinx*, or use *gypped* — Egypt). You're *punt*ing the pyramid, like a football, to see it *land* (land of Punt).

Starting in 1804, Lewis and Clark, both Americans, explored the Pacific Northwest. **Divisor** (or **dove sore** or **the visor**) would tell you 1804. Associate whichever one you're using to *loose clock* (Lewis and Clark). Link *loose clock* to an *American flag* (or a *merry can*); associate that to *pacifier* (or *specific* or *pass a fig* — whatever you conjure up that will remind you of "Pacific"); and connect that to *storm* (my standard for north — or to *Northwest* Mounted Police; or maybe just use *vest* or a *ten-gallon hat*, to remind you of "west," if that's all you need). You can apply the technique to an entire list of explorers.

Earth Science

The earth is made up of a thin outer crust, whose average thickness is 35 kilometers; the mantle, which is 2,900 kilometers deep; and the core, which has a radius of 3,470 kilometers and is made up of iron and nickel. Link *earth* to *rust* to *man tall* to apple *core*. Then, you can form separate pictures of *rust* to **mule** (or **mail** — to remind you of 35 kilometers deep); *man tall* to **nips ass** (or **no bases** — 2,900 km); and *core* to **marks** (or **my rocks** — 3,470 km) and *radios* (radius). Include *I run* (iron) and a *nickel* (the coin) if you need those reminders.

Name the major rock groups (nonmusical ones!): igneous, sedimentary, and metamorphic. Simply Link *rock* to *icky knee us* (or *egg knee us*) to *sad men tear E* to *met more fig*(s).

American History

President Grant was born on April 27, 1822, and was inaugurated president in 1869. A gigantic piece of *granite* (Grant) is placing a large **ring** (427 — April 27) on the finger of a *nun* (22). See it happening on a *ship*, as the granite takes an *oath*, and you'll know he was inaugurated president in 1869.

If you need the century, see a **tough** *nun* (1822) instead of just a nun.

Roman Numerals

D is the Roman numeral for 500. Associate **leases** (or **lasses** or **loses**) to *dean*. And moving up to 1,000:

        1 = I. Associate *tie* to *eye*.
        5 = V. Associate *law* to *veal*.
       10 = X. Associate *toes* to *eggs* (or *X-ray*).
       50 = L. Associate *lace* to *el* (elevated train).
      100 = C. Associate *disease* (or *dozes*) to *sea*.
    1,000 = M. Associate **ties sis** (or **diseases**) to *hem*.
            (Or, use a Substitute Word for "thousand";
            sand is okay — associate it to *hem* or *emperor*.)

Literature

A student of classics asked me to help him memorize the names of works that had been attributed to Plato. I needn't list them all here because it's the same sort of list I've used as an example before. The first four, in alphabetical order, were "Alcibiades," "Apology," "Charmides," and "Cratylus." The first pictures that came to my mind: *Al see a bee* in *Hades* (or *Al see a bee aid E's*); Al *apologizes* to the bee (or the bee apologizes to him); *charming D's* (or *charm hide E's* or *comedies* or *calm hides*) apologize to you; then the charming D's fly into a *crate* with an *ill ass* (*crate ill ass* — Cratylus). If this is something you need for your studies, you know where to find the other two dozen works. Just continue the Link.

Trigonometry

Some trigonometry students have told me that it would be great to know the table of trigonometric ratios; others say they would rather look up the values needed. If you choose to learn the table, I can help you do so easily. Here's part of it, to start:

r	sin r	cos r	tan r
20°	.342	.940	.364
32°	.530	.848	.625
57°	.839	.545	1.540

For each, form a Link in "degree-sin-cos-tan" order, and the problem is solved. Since you'll work in that order for each, you don't have to bother with a Substitute Word to remind you of headings; you'll know automatically which is which. Link *nose* to **marine** (or **maroon**) to **brass** to **major** (or **amateur** or **my chair**) for the first one. *Moon* to **looms** to **far off** to **channel** (the moon weaves on looms that are far off in the channel — be sure to make it ridiculous) for the second one. And, finally, **lake** to **vamp** (or **foam up**) to **laurel** to **tailors** (or **toilers** or **dollars**). That's all there is to it.

Paleontology

Another student of my systems applied them to his paleontology studies. One example is the fossil races of man — the English and Latin names.

Java Ape-man (*Pithecanthropus erectus*). An *ape* drinks *java* (coffee) like a *man*. (You could use *javelin* or *d'ja have a . . .*). The ape tries to throw a pass, but can't. He throws the ball at you and others, and he "wrecked us" (or he stands *erect*) (*Pity can't throw pass, he wrecked us — "Pithecanthropus erectus"*). *See* the picture.

Peking man (*Sinanthropus pekinensis*). See a *peeking man*. That's a *sin*, so something is *thrown* in his *puss*. That ends the *peekin'*. (*Sin and throw puss, peekin' ends*.) If your textbook uses the newer classification *homo erectus*, simply associate your Substitute Word for *that* to *peeking man*.

Heidelberg man (*Homo heidelbergensis*). A man *hides* an ice*berg* (perhaps it's *L*-shaped) in his *home*.

The *berg* falls on his *sister* and *ends* (kills) her. (*Home hide berg end sis*.)

Ngangdong man (*Homo soloensis*). A *man* falls into a pit and *no gang* will go *down* to help; he's down *so low*, the gangs go *home*.

Neanderthal man (*Homo neanderthalensis*). A *knee* and *hand* are very *tall*; the tall knee and hand go *home*.

Cro-Magnon man (*Homo sapiens*). A gigantic *chrome mug* has a *nun* in it. This chrome mug is in your *home* and you're *sippin'* from it.

After you form the associations, make a Link of the names from Java ape-man to Cro-Magnon man. That's all. Put anything else you want to know about the fossil races of man into your pictures.

Geology

It's easy to Link Substitute Words to learn the eras, epochs, and periods of earth in chronological order. One quick example: The five geologic eras all end in "zoic," so you would only have to remember the first part of the words. Start with a "heading" word for "era" (*ear* or *error*) and continue the Link to *ark keyhole* (Archeozoic) to *pro tear O* (Proterozoic) to *pail* or *pale E O* (Paleozoic) to *mess* or *mezzo* (Mesozoic) to *scene O* or *say no* (Cenozoic). These, of course, are only suggestions. You might need only *pro* to remind you of Proterozoic.

Communications

I'm including this one last section of the tablecloth chapter because it's important for you to see that memory and my systems to help you remember are useful in areas that even *I* never realized.

Marilyn Statman is the school librarian and media specialist at South Woods Middle School in the renowned Syosset School District (Long Island, New York). Through the years, I've consulted with her when there were academic situations I was called upon to solve. She uses my systems in innovative ways — such as when she teaches students to create their own television programs dramatizing the school curriculum. They develop a storyboard (a written *sequence* of scenes to be acted and videotaped), as is done for network television shows and commercials.

The point? Marilyn Statman teaches the students to select a key word or thought to represent each storyboard scene and shows them how to *Link* those scenes. She believes that paper, notes, and clipboards are distracting and time-wasting. And there *is* a time problem: a one-camera system is used and no editing is allowed; it has to be done right the first time.

I've done quite a bit of television work myself, and I've seen much time wasted looking for notes and clipboards. Marilyn Statman's idea would work as well outside of school — both in a professional television studio and in the hard-knock "real world."

Chapter 27

Graduation

• • •

*T*here's no question that the techniques, methods, systems, and ideas I've taught you in this book *work*. They've worked for many years, for literally millions of people. If you tried the ideas as you read, you know they work, and work beautifully. It's the only art/skill I know that shows results immediately, *as you learn* that skill, and it's the only one I know that will better you in a specific area even if it doesn't work!

The question, then, isn't whether or not the memory-training techniques work, but rather, how much do you want them to work for *you?* (There also is no question that whenever you remember something, you're *associating* it to something else, as you have been doing all your life — that's *how* you remember.)

It is obviously impossible to teach *everything* about the systems in a book; as I teach, I learn more that can be taught: it'd be endless. But as you use the systems, you, too, will learn; you'll see that they can be applied to any area where *learning/memory* is involved. Sure, I've used lists as some examples, and that's okay; there's much "list learning" to do for schoolwork. But if you use the techniques only for memorizing lists, you're needlessly imposing a limitation. The techniques are more important than that, and they apply to any and all learning areas. **You are limited only by your own imagination.** Using the techniques exercises that imagination as it also sharpens your observation, strengthens your concentration, and affords a greater feeling of confidence.

Well, I could go on for book after book. Just be assured that I've sold you no dreams here. I'm too result-oriented for that. Now you have an incredibly powerful weapon to use for *learning*; pick up that weapon and use it. Oh yes, it takes a bit of effort to pick it up at first. In a short while, though, you won't even think about it — just as you don't think about driving a car, typing, riding a bicycle, or ice skating: you've *forgotten* the effort that was necessary at first. And never, never lose sight of the fact that using rote memory takes *much* more effort than applying the Lorayne systems does — and isn't anywhere near as much fun or anywhere near as efficient.

You must realize this: There is *no* memory (learning) problem that you can conceivably encounter in elementary school, middle school, junior high, high school, college, or graduate school that cannot be made many times easier — and many times more fun — to solve by applying the trained-memory techniques I've taught you in this book.

Apply the techniques. Using them is probably the best investment you'll ever make — an investment that will pay dividends not only during your school years but for the rest of your life.